THE CHANGING FACE OF HONG KONG

AEI-Hoover policy studies

The studies in this series are issued jointly
by the American Enterprise Institute
for Public Policy Research and the Hoover
Institution on War, Revolution and Peace.
They are designed to focus on
policy problems of current and future interest,
to set forth the factors underlying
these problems and to evaluate
courses of action available to policymakers.
The views expressed in these studies
are those of the authors and do not necessarily
reflect the views of the staff, officers
or members of the governing boards of
AEI or the Hoover Institution.

THE CHANGING FACE OF HONG KONG

New departures in public policy

Alvin Rabushka

American Enterprise Institute for Public Policy Research
Washington, D. C.

Hoover Institution on War, Revolution and Peace
Stanford University, Stanford, California

AEI-Hoover Policy Study 6, July 1973
(Hoover Institution Studies 41)

ISBN 8447-3104-8
Library of Congress Catalog Card No. L.C. 73-84692

Printed in United States of America

For Anton

HONG KONG, KOWLOON and the NEW TERRITORIES

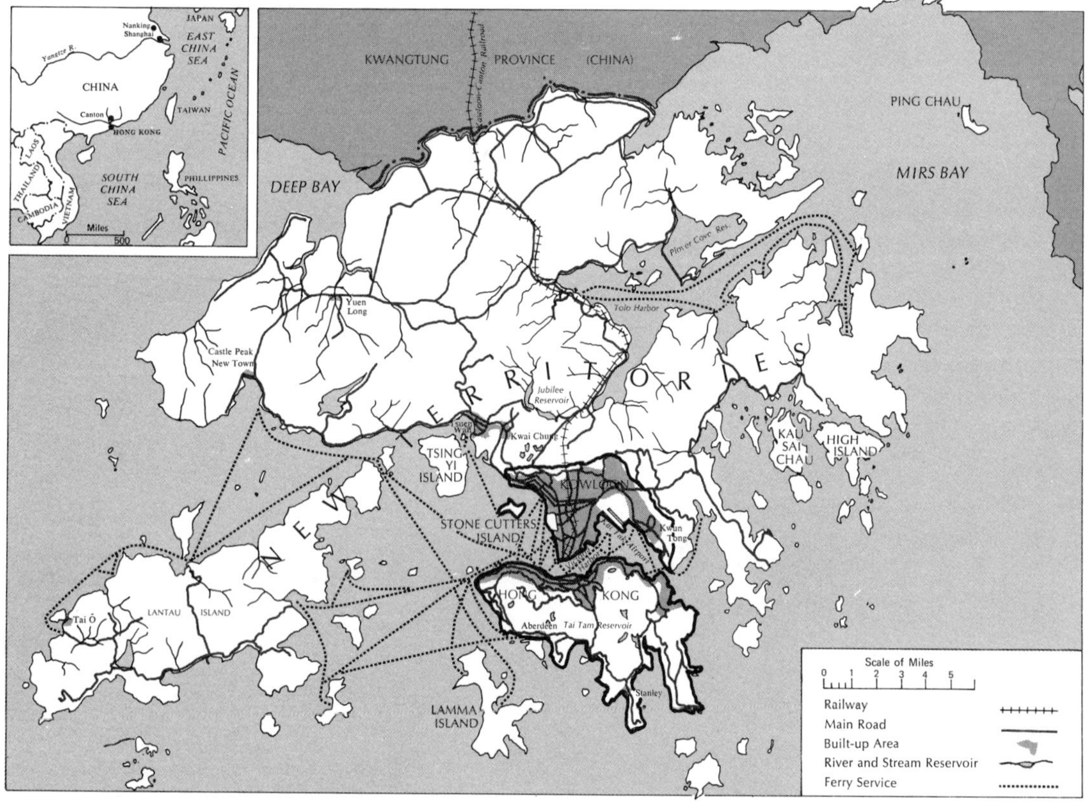

Contents

1
Introduction

This study examines the political economy of the British Crown Colony of Hong Kong. Hong Kong remains a colonial political entity, a legal condition that applies each year to a decreasing number of societies.[1] Accordingly, an investigation into the economic system of Hong Kong and the role that the Hong Kong government plays directly and indirectly in it must recognize the fact of colonial status; the colonial officials who govern Hong Kong are relatively free from the familiar demands and interests put forth by politically active citizens in independent states.

One purpose of this study is to outline the features of the twentieth century's most vivid example of a near-laissez-faire economic system, one in which government consciously restricts its economic activities. Admittedly, the retention of this free enterprise system depends heavily upon the fact of continued colonial status. Moreover, the United Kingdom bears most of the defense burden for Hong Kong—the local citizenry can conduct their economic affairs with little regard for the provision and cost of defense measures. The political realities that plague independent countries rarely preoccupy Hong Kong.

Recognizing the crucial fact that colonial status makes Hong Kong different from the independent countries in the Pacific region, it is nonetheless exciting to explore this economy on its own merits and to find out how it relates to the colonial government, because of its dra-

[1] The Bahamas, for example, received independence on July 10, 1973, and British Honduras has been scheduled for independence each year since 1968, the annual rescheduling attributable to the foreign threat posed by Guatemala. Only a few British colonial governments remain, and those which might be most amenable to comparative study with Hong Kong include Gibraltar and Bermuda. Neither of these are as yet scheduled for independence or separation from Britain.

matic postwar economic growth. However, we must be cautious in extending comparisons to other Asian countries. Given the importance of colonial status for the retention of laissez-faire, in conjunction with Hong Kong's peculiar geographical location, it would be risky to compare Hong Kong's economic prosperity to that of other Asian nations in which government takes on a much larger economic role. But the conversion of a barren rock into a dynamic economy with a rapidly rising standard of living for the ordinary citizen compels an analysis of its economic system.

Yet there is another cogent reason for serious study of Hong Kong. Its government and economy, more than any other country in the world, approximate the classical economic notion of laissez-faire that postulates a limited role for government: law and order, contract enforcement, a definition of property rights, and perhaps defense against foreign enemies. This approximation to the textbook model is, of course, made possible by the absence of an electorate and the mutual willingness of the United Kingdom and the People's Republic of China to maintain this arrangement. An analysis of the political economy of Hong Kong is therefore useful as a case study to reveal the empirical analogue to what is often put forth as an abstract textbook model with no real world counterpart. Even though the colonial government that fosters a free port in Hong Kong is not for duplication elsewhere, its mode of operation there provides an empirical illustration of how the notion of laissez-faire works in practice.

History of Statistics Collection in Hong Kong

Not only does Hong Kong's colonial status make it a very special polity, but the absence of official economic statistics makes it difficult to draw firm quantitative conclusions on the performance of Hong Kong's economy. Prior to 1947, there was no organization dealing specifically with statistical matters.[2] Population censuses were generally carried out on an ad hoc basis. Other statistics collected by government departments were the by-products of everyday work and not part of any overall statistics program. The creation of a Department of Statistics in 1947 gave priority to cost-of-living surveys, which led to monthly publication of a retail price index. Trade statistics which had been collected earlier

[2] This history can be found in *Annual Departmental Report, Commissioner for Census and Statistics (1968–69)* (Hong Kong: Government Printer, 1969), pp. 1–3.

this century prior to the 1930s and other government department information were also collected monthly and published in the statistical supplement to the Hong Kong *Government Gazette*.

The Department of Statistics was disbanded in 1952 and in its place a statistical branch was set up in the Commerce and Industry Department. Trade statistics, the retail price index, and the statistical supplement were compiled there on a routine basis. In 1959 the installation of automatic data processing equipment made it possible to improve trade statistics by separating the value of exports of Hong Kong products from that of re-exports. A household expenditure survey completed in 1963-1964 led to the replacement of the out-dated retail price index by a new consumer price index.

To prepare for the 1961 population census, the first to be taken in Hong Kong for 30 years, a separate Census Department was set up in 1959. However, immediately after the completion of the census a year later, the department was disbanded and the work of preparing population projections was transferred to the Statistical Branch of the Commerce and Industry Department.

The present Department of Census and Statistics was established in 1967; it combined the Statistical Branch, which deals mainly with economic statistics, and the Census and Statistical Planning Office, which deals with social statistics. The establishment and growth of that department has produced a marked improvement in the collection of economic and social statistics.

As indicated in the next chapter, the lack of statistics on gross national product and on earnings from invisible services and tourism, coupled with the complexities of balance-of-payments figures, restricts the confidence with which we can accept statistical accounts of Hong Kong's economic growth. However, several economists have produced careful estimates of their own and we can use these in conjunction with the available official data to present a reasonably accurate portrait of the Hong Kong economy. Moreover, the absence of official GNP statistics is, as discussed in the next chapter, an important fact.

An Overview

A primary goal of this study is to illustrate a free enterprise economy in which a postwar colonial government has played a very restricted economic role. Toward this end Chapter 2 discusses the pre- and postwar economic history of Hong Kong and elaborates upon the problems posed by the absence of systematic statistical information on Hong Kong affairs. Chapter 3 identifies the external and internal factors that condition Hong Kong's economic environment. Chapter 4 follows with an analysis of the philosophy, decision-making procedures, and economic activities carried on by the colonial government.

The final chapter focuses on recent government programs. Here several departures from the tradition of laissez-faire are itemized. Although colonial rule may be a necessary condition for the maintenance of laissez-faire in Hong Kong, it is not a sufficient condition. It may be that Hong Kong will witness the growth of restrictions on private enterprise and an expansion of government economic activity purely from internal pressures well before 1997, when the lease from China on the New Territories expires.

2
A Record of Success

The British Crown Colony of Hong Kong lies inside the tropics on the southeast coast of China, adjoining the province of Kwangtung.[1] It consists of a small part of the Chinese mainland and a scattering of offshore islands, the most important of which is Hong Kong Island. The twin cities of Victoria (on Hong Kong Island) and Kowloon (on the peninsula directly facing Victoria), which overlook Hong Kong's magnificient natural harbor, are about 90 miles southeast of Canton and 40 miles east of Portuguese Macao. Including recent reclamations, the total land area of the colony is 403.7 square miles, of which Hong Kong Island together with a number of small adjacent islands comprise 29.2 square miles. Kowloon and Stonecutter's Island comprise another 4.1 square miles. The New Territories, which consist of part of the mainland and more than 230 offshore islands, have a total area of 370.4 square miles.

Of the 403.7 square miles in the colony, only 13 percent is used for farming; 76 percent of the total area is marginal unproductive land, and the built-up areas comprise the remaining 11 percent. Within this latter 11 percent (45.7 square miles), most people live and work in 16,000 acres of extensively built-up areas (25 square miles). Moreover, the 1961 census revealed that 80 percent of Hong Kong's 3 million

[1] Much of Chapter 2 is based on material found in the *Hong Kong Annual Report,* which has been published annually since 1946. This official publication summarizes the year's developments in Hong Kong with statistical documentation where available. All money values throughout the book are in Hong Kong dollars, except where specially noted. The present parity of the Hong Kong dollar is approximately US$1.00 equals HK$5.00. That parity has varied from a high of HK$6.06 to a low of HK$5.00 during the past decade.

plus residents lived in approximately 8,000 of those acres (13 square miles), of which half is residential and a tenth industrial.

It is estimated that over 4 million people, not including the recent illegal immigrants who remain uncounted, live within these 403.7 square miles. Of these, over 98 percent can be described as Chinese on the basis of language and place of origin, of which, in turn, 55 percent are locally born, having known no home other than Hong Kong. Of the remaining 67,000 two-thirds originate from Commonwealth countries outside Hong Kong, chiefly the United Kingdom, many of whom serve in the civil service. Non-Commonwealth persons include about 6,000 Americans, and there are small Japanese, Filipino, Indonesian, Portuguese, German, Dutch, Korean, and French communities.

Throughout its history, Hong Kong has willingly accepted political refugees. Several hundred thousand entered Hong Kong in the 1930s following the start of the Sino-Japanese War in 1931. Since the end of World War II, Hong Kong's population has grown even more rapidly. When Hong Kong was liberated on 30 August 1945, after four years of Japanese rule, its population had been reduced to about one-third of its prewar size of 1.8 million. Shortly thereafter, large numbers of Chinese, whom the Japanese had forcibly deported to China during their wartime occupation of Hong Kong in order to ease the local food problems, returned at a rate approaching 100,000 a month and the population reached its prewar size by the end of 1947. Yet another influx took place during the Chinese civil war of 1948 and 1949. Nearly half a million people, mainly from Kwangtung province, Shanghai and other commercial centers, entered the colony during 1949 and the spring of 1950. Not counting returning residents, the increase in population between 1945 and 1956 due to immigration was somewhere around 1,000,000, of which some 700,000 were refugees.

The small colony of Hong Kong is almost entirely devoid of natural resources. Its mineral wealth is negligible, consisting of a modest amount of iron ore, building stone, kaolin clay, graphite, lead, and wolfram. Most of the activity in the mining and quarrying industry concentrates on the production of building stone and sand. As shown in Table 1, only one-seventh of its land is arable; the colony cannot, therefore, feed itself, and throughout most of its history has encountered difficulty in maintaining an adequate water supply. Virtually all the materials of industry and the vast majority of foodstuffs must be imported.

Hong Kong sits on the edge of an eroded mountain chain which

Table 1
LAND UTILIZATION IN HONG KONG

Class	Area (square miles)	Percentage of Whole	Remarks
Built-up (urban areas)	45.7	11.3	Includes roads and railways.
Woodlands	54.0	13.4	Natural and established woodlands.
Grass and scrub lands	233.4	57.8	Natural grass and scrub.
Badlands	14.0	3.5	Stripped of cover. Granite country. Capable of regeneration.
Swamp and mangrove lands	5.0	1.2	Capable of reclamation.
Arable	47.7	11.8	Includes orchards and market gardens.
Fish ponds	3.9	1.0	Fresh and brackish water fish farming.

Source: *Hong Kong Annual Report, 1971,* p. 65.

extends along the south coast of China, consisting mainly of sedimentary and granitic rocks. The hilly topography restricts extensive agricultural activity. In general, the shortage of land has always been one of Hong Kong's chief concerns. The island, upon its occupation by the British in 1841, had scarcely any flat land. Reporting on this condition, *The Times* (London), candidly remarked on 17 December 1844: "The place has nothing to recommend it, if we except the excellent harbor. The site of the new town of Victoria . . . is most objectionable, there being scarcely level ground enough for the requisite buildings, and the high hills, which overhang the locality, shut out the southerly winds and render the place exceedingly hot, close and uncomfortable."[2]

The colony's masters undertook reclamation within 10 years of its first occupation in 1841. Reclamation generally involves two steps. Spoil removed from quarrying and cutting back into the hills, which is an essential preparation for much of Hong Kong's building, is dumped into one of the surrounding bays; the building space is thereby extended

[2] Quoted in *Hong Kong Annual Report, 1957,* pp. 2–3. (Hereinafter cited as *Annual Report.*)

Table 2
ESTIMATED TOTAL POPULATION, 1945-1971

Mid-year	Population	Mid-year	Population
1945	600,000[a]	1959	2,967,400
1947	1,750,000	1960	3,075,300
1948	1,800,000	1961	3,168,100
1949	1,857,000	1962	3,305,200
1950	2,237,000	1963	3,420,900
1951	2,015,300	1964	3,504,600
1952	2,125,900	1965	3,597,900
1953	2,242,200	1966	3,629,900
1954	2,364,900	1967	3,722,800
1955	2,490,000	1968	3,802,700
1956	2,614,600	1969	3,863,900
1957	2,736,300	1970	3,959,000
1958	2,854,100	1971	4,045,300

[a] Rough estimate.
Source: *Hong Kong Statistics, 1947-1967* (Hong Kong: Census and Statistics Department, 1969), Table 2.2, and *Hong Kong Monthly Digest of Statistics* (Hong Kong: Census and Statistics Department, April 1972), Table 2.5.

simultaneously in two directions. The first reclamation scheme was partly completed in 1851, followed by further projects in 1867, 1884, 1885, and 1891.

Reclamation continued throughout the next 80 years; the largest schemes, totaling 415 acres, were completed around 1930. Since the war, 170 acres have been reclaimed for the Kai Tak airport, about 588 acres at Kwun Tong for private commercial, industrial, and residential development, and an additional 500 acres at Kwai Chung.[3]

Water shortages, as mentioned, have also posed severe difficulties. There are no rivers and only a few large streams in the colony. In consequence, satisfying the colony's water needs depends upon collecting and storing rainwater by systems of catchwaters and reservoirs, the bulk of which are located in the New Territories. This problem is complicated by the fact that the rainy season is concentrated in the five summer months from May to September; within these five months sufficient water must be impounded to last throughout the winter.

Between 1841 and 1863, Hong Kong Island was served by wells and hillside streams; a similar mode supplied Kowloon from 1860

[3] See *Annual Report, 1963,* pp. 28–29.

until 1910. But dependence on these sources proved risky and inadequate. Accordingly, in 1864 a reservoir was built on the island at Pok Fu Lam but it, too, soon proved inadequate. In 1889 the completion of the Tai Tam scheme increased the total storage to 312 million gallons, which was subsequently raised to 511 million gallons with the completion of the Wong Nai Chung scheme in 1899.

Across the harbor, the first reservoir was in service in Kowloon in 1910 and the opening of the Shek Li Pui reservoir in 1922 provided Kowloon with a capacity of 468 million gallons. Additional schemes in Aberdeen, the Peak, and Kowloon steadily expanded the colony's storage capacity. By World War II, the colony had 13 reservoirs that altogether could store 5,970 million gallons.

But the increasing demand for water rendered the prewar supply insufficient, leading on occasion to water rationing. At times, the mains would be opened for only three to four hours a day, or worse, for a four hour period once every four days, as in 1963. These conditions had motivated construction of the Tai Lam Chung reservoir in the New Territories which went into service in 1957 with a storage capacity of 4,500 million gallons, of Shek Pik on Lantau in 1963 with 5,390 million gallons, and of Plover Cove in the New Territories in 1969 with approximately 50,000 million gallons. Since 1968, Hong Kong has maintained a continuous water supply. To insure a steady flow for the future, the High Island scheme has commenced in the New Territories. It is scheduled for completion in 1978 with a capacity of 50,000 to 75,000 million gallons. Experimental desalinization programs have begun as well. Some of the colony's flushing and fire-fighting systems have been converted to salt water, and most new buildings are installed with salt water flushing systems. Should a new shortage develop, the colony could, by mutual agreement with China, increase its purchase of fresh water, the annual quota now being set at 18,500 million gallons.[4]

Although the water needs seem adequately provided for, Hong

[4] See *Annual Report, 1960,* pp. 7–12. An agreement to buy water from China was first concluded in 1958 for an annual quota of about 5,000 million gallons. In 1960 the annual quota was tripled to about 15,000 million gallons; this latter agreement has never lapsed. Even though Hong Kong has not always taken the full amount in years of good rainfall, by agreement it must still pay for the whole amount. This agreement is revocable by either side at a year's notice and there is provision for an additional 10 percent in any year by agreement between both parties. The present annual price of this quota is HK$17 million.

Kong still has an acute lack of suitable sites and premises for industry, with no local coal, oil, or other source of power. Nor is the colony's internal market sufficiently large to offer a solid base for economic expansion. In addition, there has been no tariff wall or other protectionist device to shield the growth of its flourishing industry from overseas competition.

Adding to the difficulties posed by overpopulation, land and water shortages, and the lack of natural resources, is the fact that Hong Kong is also in an exposed geographical and political situation, admittedly militarily indefensible. Additionally, its location presents problems of cost, market information, and cultural distance, since the United States and the United Kingdom, which together purchase 65 percent of Hong Kong's exports, are both far away. Approximately 90 percent of its manufactured goods are exported and the overwhelming bulk of its foodstuffs and consumer goods are imported. The economy is thus open at both ends and Hong Kong has little control over restrictions or quotas that other nations may implement against its goods, nor over embargoes which restrict both importing and exporting. Hong Kong at times cannot even prevent the immigration of Chinese seeking freedom and asylum. During the Korean War, for example, the United Nations embargo played havoc with the colony's economy because the entrepôt trade with China was the main part of its economy at the time. The embargo was almost a death blow to the colony's fledgling industries as well. Factories relying upon the United States for raw materials found themselves without supplies and were forced to close down.

Curiously, the Hong Kong resident, unlike the American, Englishman, Scotsman, Frenchman, Italian, or Russian, has no colloquial national designation. He is not called a Hong Kongite or Hong Kongian, but is simply a Hong Kong resident or Hong Kong born, though such designations are less awkward in the Chinese language. Little exists in the way of community- or nation-consciousness. Hong Kong Chinese regard themselves as Chinese, period. There has historically been little interest in Hong Kong politics on the part of the Chinese, who have no tradition of democratic participation and who, being largely refugees, consider the politics of the homeland to be of overriding importance.[5] Among the young, however, a Hong Kong identity has been evolving,

[5] I.C. Jarvie, "Introduction," in I. C. Jarvie and Joseph Agassi, eds., *Hong Kong: A Society in Transition* (London: Routledge & Kegan Paul, 1969), pp. xviii–xix.

especially since the riots in 1967. Many of the Hong Kong-born Chinese youth think little of mainland politics in any concrete or narrow sense.

Economic History, 1841-1941

Hong Kong became a British possession in 1841 for the simple purpose of trade with China, and prospered as a free port trading post because it offered security and freedom from interference with trade. The early inhabitants, especially the Chinese, had little or no interest in politics; the government was mainly concerned with providing a framework within which trade could flourish. At the gateway to Southern China, astride a major sea route of the Far East, Hong Kong waxed and prospered as an entrepôt, a mart and storehouse for goods in transit to Asia and the West. The colony's entrepôt character gradually diminished after World War II and the transition from entrepôt to industrial economy took place.

In keeping with Hong Kong's entrepôt character, the first industrial venture was shipbuilding and repairing. A number of ancillary industries were then established to cater to the seafaring trade: a large drydock, a sugar refinery to meet the needs of ships' procurement officers, a rope factory, and other service activities. Up until World War I the economic picture of the colony was of a number of enterprises linked with the operation of the port, with a few cottage industries. Hong Kong became the headquarters of the major merchant houses trading in the Far East. As a clearinghouse of trade between the East and the rest of the world, it soon developed specialized associated services such as banking, insurance, accountancy and legal services. It also developed special market facilities such as the gold market, to accompany shipping, which earlier had produced the related industries of shipbuilding and repairing, provisioning, wharfage and warehousing. Although the entrepôt trade with China declined after World War I, the area of the entrepôt trade grew to cover much of the Far East and Southeast Asia. Some light industry developed between the wars but it was overshadowed by the entrepôt trade.

Industrialization: Postwar Economic Growth

Manufacturing industries are today the mainstay of Hong Kong's economy. The economy is to a large extent dependent upon export-oriented light manufacturing industries and a myriad of servicing industries operating within a free port, free enterprise environment. Highly developed banking, insurance, and shipping systems inherited from the historical entrepôt era have facilitated and promoted the development of manufacturing industries. Following its entrepôt traditions, Hong Kong has no tariffs and few restrictions on the import of commercial goods. The establishment of Hong Kong as a vigorous industrial power—90 percent of manufacturing output is exported—has placed it ninth in the world in the volume of trade per capita and eighteenth in absolute terms (there are 85 recognizable countries with larger populations), and has provoked widespread attention from less successful competitors. Hong Kong has achieved this enviable record without recourse to outside economic assistance, despite formidable obstacles arising from political circumstances beyond local control.

Hong Kong's post-World War II transformation from a trading to an industrial economy was so dramatic that between 1938 and 1956 it had successfully absorbed a doubling of its population. In the wake of the war, a good many of the factors that contribute to rapid industrial development were obtained in Hong Kong almost overnight. The Communist revolution in China produced a massive influx of refugees, but most importantly, it also resulted in Shanghainese capital and entrepreneurial skill moving to the safe haven of Hong Kong. Hong Kong's industrial revolution is thus attributable to the three resources brought with the Chinese political refugees: a surplus of labor, new industrial techniques from the North, and new capital seeking employment and security. Additional circumstances favoring investment in industry included relatively high adaptability and diligence of this labor force, the weak trade union organization, the lack of legislation fixing minimum wages and limiting working hours, and the extremely low taxation on business profits. In the absence of strongly established trade unions, it became customary for individual bargains for employment to be struck, which tended to keep wage costs low. As there was also little objection to night work or to relatively long working hours, machines could be run very economically.[6] Leniency of labor regulations contributed to

[6] Nicholas C. Owen suggests that the pliant attitude of Hong Kong's labor force is due to its inability to fall back upon a rural society, which is largely nonexistent in Hong Kong. He states: "What distinguishes Hong Kong's labor force from those of neighboring countries is not its abundance but its isolation from its rural origin." See "Economic Policy in Hong Kong," in Keith Hopkins, ed., *Hong Kong: The Industrial Colony* (Hong Kong: Oxford University Press, 1971), p. 150.

labor supply being highly competitive and thus kept labor costs low.

Hong Kong's remarkable economic record is clearly revealed in its trade statistics. Although official total balance-of-payments figures are not available, the value of merchandise trade is reported. Table 3 shows that domestic exports increased at an annual average rate of 13.8 percent between 1961 and 1971. In the four years 1968-1971, the annual growth in the value of domestic exports was 25.8, 24.8, 17, and 11 percent, respectively. It is likely that industrial production grew at an annual average rate of at least 30 percent between 1950 and 1964. As a result, income figures rose faster in Hong Kong than elsewhere in Asia. It was generally accepted in 1959 that Hong Kong's industrial wages

Table 3

VALUE OF MERCHANDISE TRADE

(HK$ millions)

Year	Imports	Exports	Re-exports	Total Trade	Trade Deficit
1947	1,550	1,217	Included in Exports (1947–1958)	2,767	333
1948	2,077	1,583		3,660	494
1949	2,750	2,319		5,069	431
1950	3,788	3,715		7,503	73
1951	4,870	4,433		9,303	437
1952	3,779	2,899		6,678	880
1953	3,872	2,734		6,606	1,138
1954	3,435	2,417		5,852	1,018
1955	3,719	2,534		6,253	1,185
1956	4,566	3,210		7,776	1,356
1957	5,150	3,016		8,166	2,134
1958	4,594	2,989		7,583	1,605
1959	4,949	2,282	996	8,227	1,671
1960	5,864	2,867	1,070	9,801	1,927
1961	5,970	2,939	991	9,900	2,040
1962	6,657	3,318	1,070	11,045	2,269
1963	7,412	3,831	1,160	12,403	2,421
1964	8,550	4,428	1,356	14,334	2,766
1965	8,965	5,027	1,502	15,494	2,436
1966	10,097	5,730	1,833	17,660	2,534
1967	10,449	6,700	2,081	19,230	1,668
1968	12,472	8,428	2,142	23,042	1,902
1969	14,893	10,518	2,679	28,090	1,696
1970	17,607	12,346	2,892	32,845	2,369
1971	20,256	13,749	3,414	37,420	3,093

Source: *Hong Kong Statistics, 1947-1967,* Table 6.1 and *Hong Kong Monthly Digest of Statistics,* April 1972, Table 5.1.

were the third highest in Asia, after Japan and Singapore. They are now higher only in Japan, having doubled between 1961 and 1971.[7] A rise in local consumer prices of only 50 percent during this same period has meant a net increase of 50 percent in average real wages—a significant improvement in the standard of living of ordinary people.

Others have estimated similar rapid wage rises, but for different time spans. Henry Smith points to an average rise of 73 percent in wage rates between 1958 and 1965, an average that includes some occupations where remuneration rose more rapidly, like two-shift cotton weaving (129 percent), metal flashlight cases (123 percent), and plastics (119 percent).[8] Hughes observes that average daily wages in 1967 were double those in 1958,[9] a figure confirmed by Owen.[10]

Imports have also risen at a dramatic rate. Their 1971 value of $20,256 million was 15 percent above the 1970 figure. Foodstuffs comprised about 17 percent of all imports, with the balance consisting mainly of raw materials and semi-manufactured goods for industry, capital goods such as machinery and transport equipment, and consumer goods for both local consumption and the tourist trade. A good portion of these imports is subsequently re-exported; the value of this entrepôt trade totaled HK$3,414 million in 1971, an increase of 18 percent over 1970.

The large and growing merchandise trade deficit, which reached an all-time high of $3,093 million in 1971, is, in part, attributable to growing invisible receipts from tourism, which account for about 5 percent of gross domestic product, the earnings from services of shipping, insurance and banking, and very substantial capital inflow, all of which make possible a substantial excess of imports over exports. Indeed,

---

[7] This development—rapidly rising wages—runs counter to the prevailing beliefs of Marxist-Leninist imperialist theory, which depicts the colony as a political arrangement where the mother country can exploit the working class. The evidence of Hong Kong's doubled wages over the past decade and a net real increase in purchasing power of 50 percent confirms the opposite. Hong Kong suggests that colonial rule may not be exploiting the masses of indigenous workers. For further insights see Paul Craig Roberts and Alvin Rabushka, "A Diagrammatic Exposition of an Economic Theory of Imperialism," *Public Choice,* vol. 14 (Spring 1973), pp. 101–107.

[8] Henry Smith, *John Stuart Mill's Other Island: A Study of the Economic Development of Hong Kong* (London: Institute of Economic Affairs, 1966), p. 30.

[9] Richard Hughes, *Hong Kong: Borrowed Place—Borrowed Time* (New York: Praeger Publishers, Inc., 1968), p. 45.

[10] Owen, "Economic Policy in Hong Kong," p. 188.

earnings from these invisible services might properly be construed as the cause of the visible deficit.

The colony did not publish official estimates of national income until the printing of the *1973-74 Budget Estimates,* which contain an estimate of GNP for 1967-1971. Accordingly, earlier data that exist on the gross national product or on overall growth rates in national income are limited to scholarly estimates. K. R. Chou provides the following overall average growth rates per year in the gross national product: 1948-49, 22.6 percent; 1950-54, 5.3 percent; 1955-59, 9.0 percent; and 1960-64, 13.6 percent.[11] Szczepanik estimates the annual rates of income growth for the seven fiscal years beginning with 1947-48 as follows: 12.5, 28, 18, 0, 14, 12, and 12 percent, respectively.[12] I. C. Jarvie believes the rate of growth of the economy in the late 1960s to be in the region of 15 percent.[13] Lastly, Li and Chang consider that the growth rate averaged about 12½ percent a year between 1961 and 1968.[14]

We now have a portrait of an aggressively dynamic economy with rapid rates of overall growth, industrial productivity, and rising wages. Bank deposits also reflect this portrait. The total funds on deposit in Hong Kong banks in mid-1954 were valued at just under $1,000 million. This figure doubled by the end of 1959, doubled again by 1962, again by 1966, and still again by 1971, at which time the total on deposit exceeded $18,000 million and has grown steadily ever since. Table 4 reveals the exceptionally remarkable growth in deposits since the end of 1967, the year when the impact of the Chinese cultural revolution that spilled over into Hong Kong evaporated.

Hong Kong's economic success is also seen in the increase in the quantity of currency in circulation. An appreciation of the figures displayed in Table 5 requires an understanding of Hong Kong's currency system. The Hong Kong government does not print its own currency, and its control over the money supply operates through the use of an automatic mechanism based on the Exchange Fund Ordinance and the

---

11 K. R. Chou, *The Hong Kong Economy: A Miracle of Growth* (Hong Kong: Academic Publications, 1966), p. 81.

12 Edward Szczepanik, *The Economic Growth of Hong Kong* (London: Oxford University Press for the Royal Institute of International Affairs, 1958), p. 183.

13 Jarvie, "Introduction," in Jarvie and Agassi, eds., *Hong Kong: A Society in Transition,* p. xv.

14 N. Li and M. Chang, *Economics for Hong Kong* (Hong Kong: Longman, 1970), p. 56.

Banking Ordinance. With the exception of a small issue of coins by the government, Hong Kong's currency notes are issued by three commercial banks, the Hongkong and Shanghai Banking Corporation, the Chartered Bank and the Mercantile Bank Limited. Hong Kong does not have a central bank.

The quantity of currency issued by the note-issuing banks is regulated by the Exchange Fund, which was set up in 1935 when the Hong Kong dollar ceased to be based on silver. There is a nonstatutory agreement between government and these three private banks that they will issue currency in the equivalent amount upon the purchase with sterling of certificates of indebtedness from the government's Exchange Fund; the banks concurrently undertake to purchase or sell sterling against Hong Kong dollars within maximum exchange rate limits agreed with the Exchange Fund. Since the Exchange Fund's holdings are invested in a variety of long- and short-term sterling securities which accumulate interest, the backing of Hong Kong currency is at least 105 percent cover at the exchange rate of the day. The supply of Hong Kong currency is thus increased whenever the three note-issuing banks purchase certificates of indebtedness from government with sterling, though *in law* the financial secretary could authorize the issue of bank notes against a certificate of indebtedness without the sale of sterling, and there is authority to borrow from the Exchange Fund by exchanging the sterling backing for Hong Kong dollar government securities.

So far as the Banking Ordinance (1964) is concerned, the mecha-

Table 4

BANK DEPOSITS, 1954-1971

As of December 31	Total (HK$ millions)	As of December 31	Total (HK$ millions)
1954	1,068	1963	5,425
1955	1,137	1964	6,491
1956	1,267	1965	7,250
1957	1,412	1966	8,405
1958	1,582	1967	8,162
1959	2,055	1968	10,367
1960	2,681	1969	12,297
1961	3,367	1970	14,955
1962	4,311	1971	18,785

Source: *Hong Kong Statistics, 1947-1967,* Table 9.3 and *Hong Kong Monthly Digest of Statistics,* April 1972, Table 8.2.

nism is provided by the minimum capital and liquidity requirements, the ratio of which can be varied. The monetary system is thus automatic in that, because government is not prepared to issue short-term debt certificates, banks must look externally for the bulk of their liquid assets.

These two mechanisms largely ensure that the money supply is influenced preponderantly and over a period by the balance of payments. In practice, though not necessarily in law, the issuing of new bank notes and the expansion of deposits depend on the acquisition of external liquid assets, for example, attracting foreign funds to Hong Kong. Table 3 indicates a large deficit in the value of Hong Kong's overseas merchandise trade. This deficit is due to returns from invisible services and capital inflows, which make possible substantial imports in excess of exports. In the absence of capital inflows, a steady trade

Table 5
CURRENCY IN CIRCULATION, 1951-1971
(HK$ millions)

As of December 31	Commercial Bank Issue	Government Issue
1951 [a]	800.1	43.4
1952 [a]	801.7	41.2
1953	802.2	39.3
1954	727.5	43.4
1955	726.8	44.9
1956	731.7	51.6
1957	755.3	57.3
1958	771.9	55.7
1959	837.8	58.4
1960	913.7	70.4
1961	952.9	73.7
1962	1,045.0	78.7
1963	1,140.2	89.6
1964	1,296.5	103.0
1965	1,628.8	111.0
1966	1,730.4	122.0
1967	2,176.3	131.4
1968	1,983.6	146.9
1969	2,116.2	144.8
1970	2,413.5	164.2
1971	2,741.6	190.5

[a] As at 31 March.
Source: *Hong Kong Statistics, 1947-1967,* Table 9.1 and *Hong Kong Monthly Digest of Statistics,* April 1972, Table 8.1.

deficit would gradually reduce or eliminate from circulation Hong Kong currency, since the sterling which, in practice, provides its backing would be consumed in the settling of deficits. Although exact earnings from invisible services and tourism are unknown, they are obviously sufficient to pay for the excess of imports over exports and, as well, finance industrial expansion.

Capital inflows have been substantial throughout the postwar period. Smith calculates that foreign investment is approximately the equivalent of 20 percent of the national income of Hong Kong; he obtained these figures by projecting the rate of foreign investment required to bring about an annual rise in income of 5-7 percent after discounting domestic saving and investment.[15] Szczepanik estimates that an average surplus of approximately $400 million was built up each year on the external-payments account from 1947 to 1955, a surplus that helped finance rapid industrial development. The part played by internal savings in financing economic growth was comparatively small, approximately one-third. The remaining two-thirds was financed by capital from abroad.[16]

Chou indicates that the bulk of capital inflow, which comprised the savings of overseas Chinese, would have gone to China were it not for the political situation there. He claims that gross capital formation in Hong Kong increased from a rate of about 9 to 12 percent of gross output before 1955, to an average of 14 to 15 percent for the half-decade from 1955 to 1959, and again to that of 21 to 22 percent between 1960 and 1964. Since 1965 Hong Kong's position as a financial center in the Far East has been even more strengthened.[17]

One cannot compute the exact value of capital inflow, since neither the overall balance of payments nor the total earnings from invisible services are accurately known. But growing merchandise trade deficits and an increase in foreign exchange reserves held by banks and government imply that capital inflow and invisible earnings are large. In 1971, invisible earnings and capital inflow should approximate $4,000 million. The rate of capital inflow even appeared to rise throughout 1972. The reasons for this extraordinary rate of capital inflow are discussed in the next chapter.

---

[15] Smith, *John Stuart Mill's Other Island,* pp. 19–20.

[16] Szczepanik, *Economic Growth of Hong Kong,* pp. 142–43.

[17] Chou, *Hong Kong Economy,* pp. 6–7, and Li and Chang, *Economics for Hong Kong,* p. 66.

The economic growth of Hong Kong is also evident in the growing revenues of the Hong Kong government (Table 6). Excepting a slight increase in the 1947 earnings and profits tax rate of 10 percent to 12½ percent in 1951 and 15 percent in 1966, Hong Kong's sources of revenues and rates of taxation have remained relatively stable since 1945. Increases in revenues thus attest to a rapidly growing economy, though inflation has contributed somewhat to that increase. The administrative requirements of this burgeoning economy have also necessitated an expanding public service.

Table 6

REVENUE AND EXPENDITURE OF THE HONG KONG GOVERNMENT, 1946-1971

(HK$ millions)

Financial Year	Revenue	Expenditure	Surplus (deficit)
1946-47	82.1	85.6	(3.5)
1947-48	164.3	127.7	36.6
1948-49	194.9	150.0	35.0
1949-50	264.3	182.1	82.1
1950-51	291.7	251.7	40.0
1951-52	308.6	275.9	32.7
1952-53	384.6	311.7	72.8
1953-54	396.9	355.4	41.5
1954-55	434.5	373.3	61.1
1955-56	454.7	402.5	52.3
1956-57	509.7	469.5	40.1
1957-58	584.2	532.7	51.5
1958-59	629.3	590.0	39.4
1959-60	664.6	710.0	(45.3)
1960-61	859.2	845.3	13.9
1961-62	1,030.4	953.2	77.2
1962-63	1,253.1	1,113.3	139.8
1963-64	1,393.9	1,295.4	98.5
1964-65	1,518.3	1,440.5	77.8
1965-66	1,631.7	1,769.1	(137.4)
1966-67	1,817.8	1,806.1	11.7
1967-68	1,899.5	1,766.0	133.5
1968-69	2,081.1	1,873.0	208.1
1969-70	2,480.7	2,032.2	448.5
1970-71	3,070.9	2,452.2	618.7
1971-72	3,504.0	2,902.0	602.0

Source: *Hong Kong Statistics, 1947-1967,* Table 9.11 and *Hong Kong Monthly Digest of Statistics,* August 1972, Table 8.6.

Table 7
COST AND SIZE OF HONG KONG'S PUBLIC SERVICE, 1948-1971

Year	Authorized Size	Cost (HK$ millions)
1948-49	17,500	n.a.
1957-58	36,071	170.8
1958-59	40,429	189.5
1959-60	45,546	247.7
1960-61	50,431	285.7
1961-62	53,267	309.3
1962-63	56,910	335.6
1963-64	60,297	378.2
1964-65	63,793	457.3
1965-66	68,476	523.2
1966-67	70,853	574.0
1967-68	75,310	694.0
1968-69	77,609	796.0
1969-70	79,924	891.0
1970-71	86,268	999.0

Note: The cost of the public service has ranged between 47 and 51 percent of Hong Kong's total public recurrent expenditure.
Source: *Hong Kong Statistics, 1947-1967,* Table 9.20 and *Hong Kong Annual Reports,* 1968, 1969, 1970, 1971.

Table 7 points out the expansion in the public service from an authorized number of about 17,500 in 1949 to a present size of over 86,000 and a corresponding tenfold budget increase for personnel from less than $100 million to nearly $1,000 million.

Other signs of a rising standard of living appear in Table 8, which gives the figures for increasing electricity consumption, telephone usage, and private automobile ownership.[18] Figures on gas consumption, television ownership, and school attendance could also be marshaled to illustrate Hong Kong's postwar economic record, a story of success. To quote Nicholas Owen: "It is brilliantly successful economically, and

[18] The *Annual Reports* show that electricity prices for both the Hong Kong Electric Company and China Light and Power have steadily declined since 1946, when rates may have been fixed excessively high, while Table 8 shows steadily rising consumption. Evidently privately owned electric utilities have not extorted the consumer as some opponents of private utilities might suggest. Hong Kong may be the one society in the Far East to have suffered no serious power shortages since the end of World War II.

Table 8
MEASURES OF HONG KONG'S ECONOMIC GROWTH, 1947-1971

Year	Million Kilowatt Hours	Number of Telephones	Private Automobile Registration
1947	91.0	20,426	—
1948	150.3	21,121	—
1949	217.7	26,146	—
1950	293.5	27,761	—
1951	353.7	30,798	9,764
1952	391.4	33,9[illegible]4	11,015
1953	436.1	40,529	12,371
1954	491.6	45,829	14,500
1955	567.9	53,391	16,802
1956	649.9	61,705	19,591
1957	810.1	73,382	22,474
1958	810.1	85,391	24,378
1959	941.9	95,845	26,884
1960	1,116.0	108,799	31,507
1961	1,327.4	128,535	35,778
1962	1,537.5	145,619	40,216
1963	1,784.8	178,235	45,210
1964	2,071.6	219,693	51,073
1965	2,385.7	261,475	53,515
1966	2,710.5	301,673	56,911
1967	3,023.6	353,912	60,949
1968	3,449.5	425,000	69,062
1969	3,962.1	500,000	80,209
1970	4,450.8	580,000	92,884
1971	4,891.3	680,000	105,874

Source: *Hong Kong Statistics, 1947-1967,* Tables 5.13, 7.13 and 7.14, *Hong Kong Annual Reports,* 1968, 1969, 1970, 1971, and *Hong Kong Monthly Digest of Statistics,* April 1972, Table 6.9.

because of its free-trading *laissez-faire* system, it is unique in its correspondence to the classical economist's dream world which existed in the golden age before 1914."[19]

A Problem of Information

Hong Kong is relatively unusual in its disregard for the collection and dissemination of official economic statistics. Scholars who study the

[19] Owen, "Economic Policy in Hong Kong," p. 141.

colony often criticize government's lack of statistical bookkeeping, insisting that better bookkeeping would facilitate official and private research, and provide a framework for government planning as well.

Nicholas Owen, for one, points to this omission in his essay on government economic policy: "This account of the Hong Kong economy can now be tested. A caveat must be entered at the outset: the statistical profile of Hong Kong is so vague that no model is truly testable in Hong Kong." [20] Later in the essay he reiterates the difficulties that lack of proper information poses for the scholar: "Strangely, for a country obsessed and dominated by trade, there exist no over-all trade figures. The admirable trade statistics covering current visible trade contrast oddly with the total absence of statistics on invisibles and on capital movements. . . . As is so often the case in Hong Kong, the lack of statistics drives one to fall back on casual empiricism." [21]

John Rear, a former colleague of Owen, is even harsher in tone: "The lack of statistical information about aspects of the Colony's affairs and economy is notorious and need not be dwelt upon here." [22]

The specific types of data that are lacking are spelled out by Dwyer and Lai:

> There are almost no official figures available on the structure and performance of the Hong Kong economy apart from trade returns, and only since 1959 have the trade returns differentiated between exports of Hong Kong products and re-exports. There is no industrial census, not any officially published data upon national income, industrial costs or productivity; information on wages and hours of work is slight.[23]

They conclude their study by stating that the need of contemporary social science warrant more thorough government statistics: "Lastly, it will be obvious from the present paper that the data available on the structure and problems of the small industrial unit in Hong Kong, as of most aspects of the economy, are extremely scanty. An official approach towards the collection and publication of statistics much more

---

[20] Ibid., p. 170.

[21] Ibid., p. 183.

[22] John Rear, "One Brand of Politics," in Hopkins, ed., *Hong Kong: The Industrial Colony,* p. 66.

[23] D. J. Dwyer and Lai Chuen-yan, *The Small Industrial Unit in Hong Kong: Patterns and Policies* (Hull: University of Hull Publications, Occasional Papers in Geography No. 6, 1967), p. 11.

in keeping with the nature of contemporary research in the social sciences is needed." [24]

Richard Hughes, a long-time observer of Hong Kong, echoes similar sentiments: "The colony refuses to be bothered with official estimates of national income. Nor does it worry about balance of payments. It rolls coolly with the blows as export earnings fluctuate, and accepting any lead on points at the end of a round without elation." [25] Hughes gives an explanation for Hong Kong's statistical shortcomings, but warns that the future economic well-being of the colony may depend upon correcting these shortcomings:

> On the technical side, the colony's freebooting, free-trading traditions are mainly responsible for the distressing absence of those detailed official statistics and graphs on national income, cost and wage percentages, gross national product and growth, and all the rest of the twentieth-century economist's jargon which are now on tap at the touch of a computer button. Hong Kong has been too busy working to give proper attention to recording and codifying. This statistical deficiency is now overdue for correction. It is clear that overseas investors, who lacking the built-in confidence of overseas Chinese, want reliable data on what makes Hong Kong run, and how in fact—and reliable—it does so.[26]

In the introduction to a collection of sociological essays on contemporary Hong Kong, I. C. Jarvie notes the difficulties that the volume's contributors have confronted in quantifying their findings. He suggests, however, that official attitudes are beginning to change.

> . . . the Hong Kong government did not actively encourage or do research. A number of contributors wish strongly to emphasize that the normal aids to research were not available. The government agencies which in other places systematically gather much of the basic data from which begin many of the sorts of studies found in this book, have in Hong Kong collected (and certainly published) very little. Such collection is now beginning, but there is an almost unfillable gap left behind. To a certain extent this lack of government research stemmed from rather old-fashioned attitudes. More recently the appointment of a Commissioner of Census and Statistical Planning, and the apparent value and relative harmlessness of

[24] Ibid., p. 73.
[25] Hughes, *Hong Kong: Borrowed Place—Borrowed Time,* pp. 17–18.
[26] Ibid., pp. 48–49.

such research as has been done already, seems to have overcome these attitudes.[27]

Why are academics nearly unanimous in their demand for more official statistics in Hong Kong? For one thing, publication of accurate information would facilitate contemporary social science research in such quantitatively oriented fields as economics, sociology, and political science. More to the point, it is impossible for government to undertake an economic planning role for the society if it does not know the society's current economic performance. On what baselines can a five-year plan be developed? How can one project the future gross national product if present GNP is unknown? Most academics assign to government, in Hong Kong as elsewhere in the world, a major responsibility for guiding and encouraging economic growth, and this responsibility cannot be discharged in statistical ignorance. A specialist on Hong Kong land use, T. R. Tregear, rationalizes his motives for government interference in economic affairs:

> Whether we like it or not, we live in an era of "planned economy." For a number of reasons, not least the growth of world population, we have left behind us the *laissez-faire* of the nineteenth century. Modern society is complex. Its activities are so interwoven and often, maybe, conflicting, that some sort of planning and organization by government authorities is essential. Planning and forethought in the use of our land has all too often been left too late. When the planners have come into the field, they have found their work complicated and sometimes impossibly compromised by rule of thumb development which has already taken place. Land suited to residential uses has been spoilt by factories and workshops; slum areas allowed to develop; roads and communications jeopardized and made expensive in development by unwise and thoughtless building; agricultural land spoilt by careless granting of mining rights and so on.[28]

In 1962, the government of Hong Kong commissioned E. R. Chang to conduct a survey of the colony's national income to derive statistics therefrom in a form suitable for publication, and to lay the foundation for their continuing review in a practicable manner. What is the value

[27] Jarvie, "Introduction," in Jarvie and Agassi, eds., *Hong Kong: A Society in Transition,* p. xxi. The harmlessness and apparent value of these statistics are not quite so evident for reasons that follow.

[28] T. R. Tregear, *Land Utilization in Hong Kong* (Hong Kong: Hong Kong University Press, 1955), p. 1.

of national income estimates, we might ask, apart from being an aid to scholarly research? Chang indicates four distinct areas of policy in which social accounting can be of use: (1) policy affecting the size and distribution of the national income, (2) policy affecting the efficient allocation of the resources of the economy, (3) policy affecting the rate and direction of the nation's economic growth, and (4) policy affecting economic stability. Note, however, that national income accounting is useful in throwing light on policy decisions only insofar as these decisions imply some form of value judgment based on welfare and productivity. National income accounting was originally developed for these purposes, and the collection and publication of national income statistics imply an official interest in the distribution of national income. Note also that national income accounting is useful to policy makers if they seek to play a role in evaluating competitive claims on the scarce resources of the economy, and thereby allocating those resources to meet the government's specified goals for the economy. It is not clear, therefore, that national income statistics would be of much use to policy makers in Hong Kong's traditionally laissez-faire environment.

Moreover, in the absence of exchange controls, a fact contributing to the magnetic attractiveness of Hong Kong as a financial center, it would be difficult to compile accurate balance-of-payments accounts. Although Chang recommends that the government give high priority to producing regular estimates of balance-of-payments accounts, he points to the practical problems in accurate estimation:

> The need for balance of payments accounts in a country which is so dependent on the international sector, should be fairly obvious. There are many difficulties in initiating such a system of accounts, foremost among these is the difficulty of obtaining adequate statistics. Most countries keep proper statistics on the import and export of merchandise. It is the so-called "invisible" imports and exports which pose the greatest problem. This is partly due to the fact that records of imports and exports of merchandise are usually kept for administrative purposes, e.g., the levy of customs duties. On the other hand, the greater part of the "invisible" exports and imports is seldom subject to official scrutiny, except in cases where regulations like exchange control require it. With these exceptions the availability of statistics on "invisible" items depends on the willingness of the private sector to give them. For obvious reasons the private sector is unwilling to do so. Considerable pressure may be needed to obtain the required

statistics. The need for balance of payments data is too pressing to allow the difficulty of obtaining statistics to deter a country from initiating the preparation of these accounts.[29]

Hong Kong's money supply, merchandise trade, and government reserves have grown in the absence of any balance-of-payments accounts. Hong Kong's success clearly demonstrates that these accounts are *not* necessary for economic growth. Indeed, the contrary may be true. Interference by government in business, requiring the provision of financial data, may discourage, obstruct, or slow down the sustained and rapid economic growth rate of the past decades. Is it possible then that the "pressing need" for balance-of-payments accounts and the like is ideological rather than practical?

The attitude of the Hong Kong government toward the collection and publication of such statistics as gross national product and balance of payments is very clear. The remarks of the financial secretary, Sir John Cowperthwaite, before the Hong Kong Legislative Council in March 1970 typify this attitude:

> There was a plea from honorable Members relating to the need for formal Gross National Product figures. Such figures are very inexact even in the most sophisticated countries. I think they do not have a great deal of meaning, even as a basis of comparison between economies. That other countries make use of them is not, I think, necessarily a good reason to suppose that we need them. But, although I am not entirely clear what practical purpose they would serve in Hong Kong, I am sure they would be of interest. I suspect myself, however, that the need arises in other countries because high taxation and more or less detailed Government intervention in the economy have made it essential to be able to judge (or to hope to be able to judge) the effect of policies, and of changes in policies, on the economy. One of the honorable Members who spoke on this subject said outright, as a confirmed planner, that he thought that they were desirable for the planning of our future economic policy. But we are

[29] E. R. Chang, *Report on the National Income Survey of Hong Kong* (Hong Kong: Government Printer, 1969), p. 93. Assume the government extracted earnings from invisible services and tourism under threat of law, and attempted to distinguish between the bank accounts of residents and nonresidents. These data would be very inaccurate. It is well known that most firms keep two sets of books, one for the Inland Revenue Department and the other for the owners. Also, capital from abroad is often sent to a family member, a resident of Hong Kong, who then deposits it in his own account. Thus, the overall balance-of-payments figures would be highly inaccurate and of little value to government.

in the happy position, happier at least for the Financial Secretary, where the leverage exercised by Government on the economy is so small that it is not necessary, nor even of any particular value, to have these figures available for the formulation of policy. *We might indeed be right to be apprehensive lest the availability of such figures might lead, by a reversal of cause and effect, to policies designed to have a direct effect on the economy. I would myself deplore this.*

The other concern seems rather to be for our international prestige. If we had formal GNP statistics, I suppose we could boast of our economic progress in more precise and authoritative, even if not very accurate, figures and thereby prevent others from belittling us; but I cannot see any great value in that. It is the fact of our progress that is important.

My honorable friend, Mr. Wilfred Wong, remarked that we have not yet heard from the University fellow appointed to study the question. In fact his report was published in December last year; . . . My own conclusion from the report is that the expense and effort needed to produce even very approximate figures in our free economy outweigh the value of having them. As to cost, about which my honorable friend Dr. Chung enquired, the report suggests a figure of $250,000 a year for basic salaries alone at the 1967 levels. Today, I suppose the total cost would be of the order of $500,000 a year. But the budgetary cost is only a small part of the story; I doubt if our friends in commerce, finance, the professions, etc., would relish the form-filling that would be necessary; for their time is also money. . . .

But I feel myself that, in Hong Kong, GNP and other national accounts are a proper subject for academic rather than official research; as it was indeed in other countries at a time when the relationship of Government to the economy was not dissimilar from ours today.[30] (Italics supplied.)

In this revealing speech, Sir John Cowperthwaite, generally regarded to be the dominant figure in the economic activities of the Hong Kong government throughout the 1960s,[31] expressed the fear that the very existence of national accounts statistics might encourage government to assume a direct planning role and interfere in the private sector with counterproductive results. The absence of such statistics guards against the temptation for government planning.

---

30 *Hong Kong Hansard 1970,* pp. 495–96.
31 See Rear, "One Brand of Politics," p. 65.

One additional statement by Sir John Cowperthwaite, a portion of an interview published in *The Banker,* deserves note.

> *Question:* One thing that seems rather surprising to the outside observer is the paucity of economic statistics for Hong Kong. While trade statistics are good, there seem to be no proper balance-of-payments figures, nor those for the Gross National Product. Why is this?
>
> *Answer:* The simple answer is that we have *no practical use* for them and are not prepared to go to the expense and trouble (not least on the part of businessmen and bankers who have more important things to do) of collecting them, if indeed they are collectable here even to the rather inaccurate standards of other countries; just for the purposes of historical record or international league tables. With our total dependence on foreign trade, our balance-of-payments must be, by and large, automatic and the system reacts long before any figures could be put together. Indeed, one may go further and say that the balance-of-payments is a cause, not an effect, of monetary conditions.
>
> So far as the Gross National Product is concerned, it is one of the benefits of a necessarily low taxed economy that the demands of public spending are not constantly pressing on the resources of the country in a more or less inflationary way. That being so, GNP statistics are of no practical use. I am much more immediately interested in growth of fiscal revenues than in GNP: in our economy, of course, there is a correlation between them but the tax returns are likely to come in before the GNP statistics. This does not mean we do not have some idea of GNP; the question is how far it is worth refining it.
>
> Trade statistics, of course, are different, not so much for the aggregate figures, but for the detailed information on trade developments which are useful to businessmen. They are also, I am sorry to say, essential material in trade negotiations, not, I hasten to add, for purposes of bilateral trade agreements, but for negotiations on restrictions other countries regrettably wish to place on our trade.[32]

Sir John Cowperthwaite was replaced as financial secretary on July 1, 1971, by Charles Philip Haddon-Cave. The change in personnel has produced a shift in the official attitude toward national accounts statistics. To the delight of the social scientists and the dismay of advocates of strict laissez-faire, the Hong Kong government now collects

[32] July 1970, pp. 741–42.

national accounts statistics.[33] It is clear that the prior lack of statistics was due to the vigorous objections of Sir John Cowperthwaite and that the new policy is traceable to his successor. Whether the collection of statistics foreshadows a larger role for government economic planning is discussed in Chapter 5.

[33] Interview with Financial Secretary Charles Philip Haddon-Cave, June 22, 1972. It is interesting that the social scientists studying Hong Kong have unanimously indicted the government's policy towards the collection and publication of statistics. In the author's view, this pattern is suggestive of the values and political preferences of these scholars.

3

The Economic Environment

Hong Kong's remarkable postwar economic growth is due, in large measure, to factors outside its borders over which it has little or no control. The colony depends for its survival chiefly upon exports and imports, especially capital. Domestic factors also play an important role, however, for they create the environment conducive to economic prosperity.

External Factors

The history of Hong Kong is, in some ways, a chronicle of rising and falling trends of trade and population, responding in the main to events taking place abroad, particularly in China. Hong Kong's rapid population increase between 1945 and 1956, for instance, is largely attributable to a massive exodus of refugees from China who sought freedom and asylum in Hong Kong. The wave of illegal immigration in 1962 seems not to have been discouraged in its early stages by the Chinese authorities, and what their future policies on illegal immigration might be are unknown. Industrialization in Hong Kong is also directly due to the inflow of a large labor force, plus industrial know-how and capital, during the turbulent years of 1949-1950. Thus industrialization and rising population resulted from factors largely outside Hong Kong's control.

The greater part of Hong Kong's territory is leased from China. The New Territories, signed over to Britain in 1898 on a 99-year lease, are due to be returned to China on the expiration of the lease in 1997. Hong Kong Island, Kowloon, and Stonecutter's Island, the remaining territories that were ceded to Britain in perpetuity, are not politically or economically viable as a separate unit. Without water and industry, which are mainly located in the New Territories, the foundation for Hong Kong's economic prosperity will disappear.

Until 1997, Hong Kong survives on China's tolerance—on the gains from trade that make its continued existence worthwhile to China. The latter needs foreign exchange. Since the mid-1960s, receipts from Hong Kong are believed to have run annually in the hundreds of millions of dollars and to have accounted for some 40 percent of China's total earnings of foreign exchange. Much of this is earned by the sale of water, food, and basic necessities to the colony. Ironically, these basic necessities, imported into Hong Kong at low prices, have reduced the pressure upon industrialists to pay higher wages. China almost appears to be subsidizing Hong Kong industry.[1]

Although Hong Kong's economy is now based on exports of manufactures, its preindustrial economy depended heavily on the entrepôt trade with China. This dependence nearly proved fatal in 1950 at the outbreak of the Korean War. The United States embargo cut off supplies to newly established industrial plants in Hong Kong and many were forced to close down. A United Nations embargo on China, which Hong Kong honored, cut the level of the colony's trade considerably. America's withdrawal of the embargo on Hong Kong and the rapid establishment of an export-oriented industrial sector forestalled an economic collapse. Now export trade to China is but a mere fraction of its previous levels.

The importance of China to Hong Kong's welfare was underscored during the now-famous 1967 riots. These riots stemmed directly from the Chinese cultural revolution, which instilled in its adherents a fervent patriotism and an adulation for Chairman Mao Tse-tung. Hong Kong became an obvious target for this missionary zeal. Although the less fanatical among the Communists were concerned over the possible loss of the economic advantages that a stable and prosperous Hong Kong has for China, they could not oppose confrontation without appearing to oppose the teachings of Chairman Mao. The Hong Kong government, following the wishes of the bulk of the local citizenry, held firm and fully reestablished its control during the summer of 1967.[2]

---

1 Joe England, "Industrial Relations in Hong Kong," in Hopkins, ed., *Hong Kong: The Industrial Colony,* p. 217.

2 *Annual Report, 1967,* pp. 1–21.

But the riots revealed Hong Kong's vulnerability to developments in China that may spill over into Hong Kong. Many in the colony assert that Peking can recover Hong Kong for the price of one phone call, preferably with a courteous few weeks advance notice.

China is no longer dominant as an export market, having been superseded by the United States and Great Britain, which, respectively, take 42 percent and 14 percent of all Hong Kong exports by value.[3] Nonetheless Hong Kong's future continues to lie in external hands, for the possible imposition of tariffs and quota orders by the countries importing the colony's industrial products has become the biggest threat to its continued economic growth.

As the United Kingdom has acceded to the General Agreement on Tariffs and Trade (GATT) on behalf of Hong Kong, the colony's exports are given most-favored-nation tariff treatment in the majority of its overseas markets and are accorded a degree of protection against discriminatory import restrictions by members of GATT. Hong Kong is designated as a beneficiary of the various preference schemes established by the European Economic Community (EEC), Japan, Norway, New Zealand, and Sweden. Nevertheless, its leading exporters still voice concern over Britain's joining the European Common Market.

Under existing EEC-Hong Kong arrangements, the colony has agreed to hold exports of some finished fabrics and made-ups and apparel items to agreed limits. But restrictions placed upon its exports by the United States, its largest market, are potentially more troublesome. Exports of cotton textiles to the United States are now restrained under a three-year agreement which commenced on October 1, 1970. The limit for the textile year 1970-71 allowed such exports to rise 5 percent above the previous year's level. Under another agreement signed in early 1972, Hong Kong agreed to restrain its exports of wool and man-made fibers textiles to the United States for a period of five years. A last example is found in the reintroduction by the United States of a tariff-rate quota for certain low-price stainless steel flatware, now fixed at 1.5 million pieces, with a small annual growth. Exports in excess of the quota are subject to prohibitive rates of duty.

The effect of these various quotas, tariffs, and other restrictions is the limitation of potential growth in the volume of specific kinds of exports to Hong Kong's chief overseas market to a fixed, agreed-upon

---

[3] *Annual Report, 1971,* p. 27.

percentage. Moreover, within Hong Kong, American quotas imply unfair advantage for the larger well-established firms for whose goods the quota will be allocated. Free from domestic competition, these firms, in effect, are guaranteed a minimum market in the United States which they will be likely to fill with higher priced goods than before. Domestic competition in Hong Kong will no longer serve to keep down the prices of these goods.

Political instability and corruption throughout the rest of Asia represents yet another external factor affecting Hong Kong's well-being. Capital inflows into Hong Kong often account for 20 percent of its national income and have financed at least two-thirds of its economic expansion. It is believed that the bulk of this money consists of the savings of the overseas Chinese who might have sent their money to China had conditions been different there. Foreign money is still flowing into Hong Kong and its continued flow is judged essential to maintain a high rate of economic growth in the colony.

Exact figures on capital inflow are unknown because Hong Kong does not have an exchange control system which differentiates between resident and nonresident accounts. Moreover, banks cannot in practice determine in many cases whether deposits are resident-owned or not. Some have estimated that as high as 50 percent of the total value of bank deposits come from outside. Indeed, the colony's liberal exchange control system, convertibility of currency, and security for capital will continue to encourage this inflow so long as other Asian nations remain susceptible to chronic instability or rampant corruption. If the postwar era is at all indicative of the future, capital inflows will continue to enrich Hong Kong.

Internal Factors

Domestic considerations also play an important role in the colony's prosperity. If Hong Kong mirrored the instability and corruption so characteristic of many of its Asian neighbors, refugee labor, entrepreneurs, and capital would not be lured to Hong Kong. But around a large, landlocked, deep-water harbor, Hong Kong's rulers have fashioned an environment conducive to economic prosperity.

Richard Hughes, a noted journalist, puts the Hong Kong formula for success in simple and straightforward language: low taxes, quick profits (investments are usually amortized in three to five years), hard work, and, most important, laissez-faire.[4] Giving this view academic rationalization, Professors Li and Chang cite the benefits of free trade for Hong Kong: "Hong Kong is well known throughout the world as a free port where its people pay homage to the principles of free unhampered international trade . . . it is a fact that an economic society is always *more efficient under free trade* than it is when there are trade barriers inter-regionally or internationally." [5] (Italics supplied.)

Unlike most of the new but backward countries that appeal to national pride to urge greater output from their citizens, Hong Kong as a colony depends strictly on the individual profit motive:

> *Laissez-faire* capitalism is another institutional datum of the utmost importance for understanding the recent growth of Hong Kong's economy. The Colony was founded as a free port and this idea has remained almost unchanged. Economic liberalism extends, of course, not only to foreign trade but also to all internal economic activities: production, transport, exchange, and finance. The economic development of Hong Kong has not been directed by any overall national plans. Instead of appeals to national pride or imposition of overriding national aims to benefit future generations, self-interest has been the prime mover of Hong Kong's economic growth.[6]

Hong Kong's few trade controls are exceedingly simple, especially when they are compared with the contemporary restrictionist world. Virtually complete freedom from trade controls is deemed central to the success of Hong Kong's continuing industrial revolution. This near laissez-faire has unleashed human potentialities which in other countries remain paralyzed by elaborate control systems. The Hong Kong investor enjoys the benefits of a free market in foreign exchange, freedom from the political and racial discrimination—especially against Chinese—so often found among its Southeast Asian neighbors, and immunity from official controls and interference. Moreover, in the absence of import controls, industry is not protected from overseas competition and must prove itself by its own efficiency. Hong Kong has no general tariff or protective duties: "In these circumstances it seems likely that the policy of laying as little restraint as possible on the profit-seeking entrepreneur will have conduced to a greater reduction in unemployment

---

[4] Hughes, *Hong Kong: Borrowed Place—Borrowed Time,* p. 17.

[5] Li and Chang, *Economics for Hong Kong,* p. 57.

[6] Szczepanik, *The Economic Growth of Hong Kong,* p. 7.

and rise in real wages than a policy that brought some immediate relief and protection to the wage earner in his working life, but by regulations that impeded enterprise." [7]

Laissez-faire means in practice that the setting up of a business enterprise is not impeded by government. The principle of free entry into almost every line of production is rigorously enforced. The legal formalities required to set up a business, even to establish a private company, are for the most part, few and inexpensive—the Business Registration Ordinance of 1952 reduced the annual fee for a business license from $200 to $25, exempting certain small or dormant businesses from the fee altogether. For approximately five American dollars, one can lawfully open a business in Hong Kong.

Nor do high taxes impede the establishment of enterprise or dampen the profit motive. The standard tax on profits and earnings was levied at a flat rate of 10 percent in 1947, raised to 12½ percent in 1951 and finally to 15 percent in 1966. Unincorporated businesses are assessed only on the excess of their annual profits over $7,000. But it is generally recognized that the account books shown to Inland Revenue reveal some, not all, of the total earnings of most businesses. Government staff available for inspection is small relative to the number of establishments and they are not severe in their enforcement of the tax laws (so long as government revenues and surpluses keep rising).

Leniency of labor regulations also encourages enterprise, causing wage rates to reflect market conditions, not arbitrary bureaucratic judgments. There are neither minimum wages nor restrictions on the working hours of men in industry. Some recent legislation has intensified the regulation of certain types of labor conditions in Hong Kong (see Chapter 5), but the Department of Labor is also overburdened (or understaffed), which means that many of the colony's labor laws are not rigidly enforced.

Hong Kong, today, is a completely free market in money. No barriers restrict exchange between the Hong Kong dollar and other currencies. Nor does government distinguish between resident and nonresident accounts for exchange control or tax purposes. Hong Kong is thus a genuine financial haven—financial assets are easily transferable or convertible with minimum regulation or interference. The ever-increasing

[7] E. H. Phelps Brown, "The Hong Kong Economy: Achievements and Prospects," in Hopkins, ed., *Hong Kong: The Industrial Colony*, p. 9.

funds that have been attracted to Hong Kong banks helped finance industrial development. Hong Kong is essentially laissez-faire—a free port governed by a liberal import regime, almost no significant impediments to the establishment of business, low rates of taxation on earnings and profits, liberal exchange control requirements, and lenient labor regulations.

Laissez-faire has remained the general policy of the Hong Kong government—to intervene as infrequently as possible in the process of industrialization. Thus no special official provision, financial or physical, is made either for individual types of industry or size of industrial units. In only two instances has official intervention been occasioned, and those only to regulate the allocation of extremely scarce industrial land: "First, the government has reserved certain coastal sites for such industries as electricity generation, boat building and shipbreaking. Secondly . . . some small industrial units have come within the scope of the government's policy of large scale squatter resettlement and as a result have been rehoused."[8]

The fact that laissez-faire has proved so rewarding in Hong Kong stems from the provision of political stability by the Hong Kong government, an environment free from violent social and political upheaval. "Basic administration is competent and thorough: perhaps, by Asian standards, admirable."[9] "It remains impressively true that Her Majesty's Government in Hong Kong for all its colonialism and stuffiness has a much better record of preserving public order and personal freedom than most governments, or any government, in Asia."[10] The investment capital which Hong Kong attracts from all over Southeast Asia is due, in large measure, to its exceptional political stability. Following is a description of the Hong Kong government's competence and efficiency:

> By all visible signs, the colony is one of the best-run governments in the Far East. Its roads are paved and traffic moves in an orderly way in spite of the highest vehicle concentration per mile of road anywhere in the world. The same order prevails in the incessant shuttling of harbor vessels. Public transportation is swift, frequent and generally on schedule. Poverty and privation are everywhere, but starvation is virtually non-existent. Business and trade thrive and unem-

---

[8] Dwyer and Lai, *Small Industrial Unit in Hong Kong,* p. 23.
[9] Rear, "One Brand of Politics " p. 121.
[10] Keith Hopkins, "Preface," in Hopkins, ed., *Hong Kong: The Industrial Colony,* pp. xiii–xiv.

ployment is low. Wages seem miniscule when compared with American standards, yet are higher than in most of the countries of Asia. A majority of its people are indifferent to the government, but they are not afraid of it. When something has to be done, there are people at the top with the resolution and intelligence to do it without trampling human rights.[11]

The government can also be credited with having done much to develop the infrastructure for industry. Without government's great achievement in rehousing more than one million refugees (see Chapter 4), the development of an efficient industrial labor force would hardly have been possible. It has also facilitated the acquisition of factory sites by vast reclamations (a major problem in the terrain of Hong Kong) and has provided factory premises to rent for the resettlement of squatter factories. The government in general capably provides law and order, water supplies, roads and town planning, in addition to site formation for industrial, commercial and residential purposes. As Nicholas C. Owen has pointed out, "What needs to be observed here is not that these functions are performed, since all governments take responsibility for these basic functions, but that they are performed with a competence rare in South Asian cities."[12]

By modern standards, Hong Kong follows a prudent, almost Gladstonian, fiscal policy. It does not contribute to inflation by following the current practice of deficit spending so prevalent among most governments. Prudent fiscal policy conjoined with low rates of taxation instills a genuine air of business confidence in the Hong Kong government. Though some corruption no doubt exists, it is very well contained, and far less disruptive of economic activity than elsewhere in the Far East.[13] The colony is known for its large narcotics problem, with guesses that range as high as 80,000 addicts (2 percent of the total population). Gambling and prostitution are also widespread, but again under control, and do not becloud the economic picture.

---

[11] Gene Gleason, *Hong Kong* (New York: The John Day Company, 1963), pp. 216–17.

[12] Owen, "Economic Policy in Hong Kong," p. 156.

[13] For a provocative treatment of the problem of corruption in Hong Kong see Elsie Elliott, *The Avarice, Bureaucracy and Corruption of Hong Kong* (Hong Kong: Friends Commercial Printing Factory, 1971). Another discussion is found in Chapter 7 of Gleason's book, *Hong Kong*. Those readers with sufficient background in Hong Kong affairs will find reading between the lines in the cases reported in the *Annual Report of the Umelco Office, Hong Kong* extremely informative.

Political security, orderly administration, and a near laissez-faire policy have combined to create an environment conducive to the success of skilled entrepreneurship. As already noted, extremely favorable circumstances for investment in industry include a highly capable and diligent labor force as well.[14] Hong Kong had a higher percentage of its labor force in industry in 1966 than any other Asian country. Between 1961 and 1969 the number of industrial undertakings increased seven times over, and the employment they gave increased by 600 percent. Indeed, industry has grown so rapidly that certain kinds of labor are in short supply and industrial wages have risen reflecting an improved seller's market in labor. Legislation fixing minimum wages does not exist and severe restrictions on working hours for women and children are a relatively new innovation.

Entrepreneurs have not had to cope with strong trade unionism. The percentage of employees whom the unions claimed to be members was about 12 percent in 1966, although the figure is closer to 20 percent for those in full-time employment. Moreover, this figure is probably an exaggeration.[15]

Trade unionism is not only weak but is growing weaker in proportion to the working population. Average membership declined by 24,000 between 1961 and 1969 while the labor force increased by 288,000. In manufacturing, unions have organized no more than 6.5 percent of the working force, and these are chiefly in the old industries of shipbuilding, food, furniture, and woodwork. Unions are virtually nonexistent in the large and dynamic industries.

Weak trade unionism is attributable to political factors. Most workers' unions are either affiliated to, or associated with, one of two local federations—the Communist Hong Kong Federation of Trade Unions (FTU) or the right-wing Hong Kong and Kowloon Trades Union Council (TUC)—which are registered as societies and not as trade unions, and which bear allegiance to opposing political groups. In addition, there are 73 politically uncommitted unions which consist mainly of white-collar workers including many government and armed service employees. In 1969, 65 unions were affiliated to the Communist FTU and another 16 considered sympathetic. These unions organized

[14] Judith Agassi, "Social Structure and Social Stratification in Hong Kong," in Jarvie and Agassi, eds., *Hong Kong: A Society in Transition*, p. 67.

[15] England, "Industrial Relations in Hong Kong," p. 237. This discussion on labor is based on England's presentation.

workers in public utilities, transport, shipyards, textile mills, and merchant shipping. The right-wing TUC in 1969 had 68 affiliates and some 31 sympathetic unions, active mainly in building construction, restaurants, textiles, and a number of small trades and industries. All together, 57 percent of trade unionists were in unions supporting the People's Republic of China and 19 percent in unions sympathetic with the government in Taiwan.

Political divisions among trade unionists weaken the trade union movement. Too many unions with too few members also contribute to fragmentation. Reflecting this weakness, most formal rules governing work and employment relationships are made unilaterally by the employer—collective bargaining in Hong Kong applies to under 5 percent of all employees. In most large manufacturing industries trade unions are extremely weak, and, in any case, rising real wages and expanding job opportunities—the pressure of market forces—which permit a high turnover of labor in manufacturing enterprises, would have rendered unions irrelevant to workers' improved welfare.

The importance of enterprise as a factor of production must itself not be overlooked. The arrival in 1949 and 1950 of Shanghainese with their entrepreneurial skills and knowledge of modern industrial techniques facilitated the colony's industrial revolution. Professors Li and Chang emphasize the importance of this enterprise to a dynamic economy.

> In a free-enterprise economy, enterprise as a factor of production is especially important. The rewards of enterprise, or the desire for profit, is a great force in coaxing out entrepreneurial ability from the citizens. If a country is run on a dictatorial basis, the amount of enterprise supplied by its citizens will dwindle and decline. In a *laissez-faire* economy like Hong Kong with a population full of resourcefulness and rich in business initiative, we are particularly fortunate in our endowment of enterprise as a factor of production.[16]

Although the following passage was written in 1958, this description of Hong Kong still aptly suits 1973.

> . . . the existence of stable government, which has provided an atmosphere of peace and security, free from violent social and political upheavals; the attraction of capital into the Colony, particularly from areas in South-East Asia shaken by

[16] Li and Chang, *Economics for Hong Kong,* p. 35.

discord; a deeply-rooted tradition of efficiency in such services as banking, shipping and insurance, all of them vital to industrial growth; a large merchant community with trading links all over the world; a sheltered, deep-water harbor; the existence of an abundant, hard-working and adaptable labor force; an influx from the Chinese mainland of skilled workers and industrialists, some of them with considerable capital and knowledge of modern techniques; and the advantages deriving from the Colony's place in the Commonwealth. To these should be added a strong faith in the merits of free enterprise and least possible interference by the Government in trade and industry; a wholesome respect for the profit motive; and relative freedom from stoppages of work and other forms of industrial dispute.[17]

[17] *Annual Report, 1958,* pp. 2–3.

4
The Hong Kong Government

Upon the ratification of the Nanking Treaty on 26 June 1843, a colonial administration was set up in Hong Kong. Although Hong Kong had been occupied in January 1841, the British government had refused in the interim to acknowledge its official occupation of the territory in the absence of a treaty. But very soon thereafter, the colony began to play an influential role in the China trade and quickly supplanted Macao, which lacked a comparable deep-water harbor. A substantial foreign community was readily attracted into Hong Kong, and it rapidly outnumbered the foreign community of traders still resident in Canton. Early Hong Kong was thus cosmopolitan for "it was the deliberate policy to attract all comers to the port without distinction of race in accordance with the liberal character of British economic policy of this period." [1] From the very outset, however, Chinese heavily outnumbered the foreigners.

The opium trade, which motivated both the seizure and colonization of Hong Kong, gave rise to an unruly community of residents and crime immediately became prevalent. The first urgent problem of the Hong Kong government, then, was to maintain minimal law and order and give protection for person and property.

Lord Stanley, secretary of state for war and the colonies during this period (1841-1845), expressed his views on Hong Kong in a letter to Hong Kong's first governor, Sir Henry Pottinger: the function and purpose of Hong Kong was to serve as a diplomatic, commercial, and

---

[1] G. B. Endacott, *Government and People in Hong Kong* (Hong Kong: Hong Kong University Press, 1964), p. 15. The first portion of Chapter 4 is condensed, in large measure, from Endacott's book.

military post.[2] Pottinger was instructed on three accounts: (1) to negotiate with the Chinese emperor, (2) to superintend the trade of British subjects in China, and (3) to regulate the internal trade of the settlement. The specific constitutional arrangements drawn up for Hong Kong reflected the special conditions of British activity in the Far East, where a great degree of central control would prove advantageous. Hong Kong was, at the outset, a barren island with no large or old-established community entitled to political representation. It was essentially a military, diplomatic, and trading station, not a settlement in the normal sense, and strategic empire considerations demanded firm imperial control.

Administrative absolutism meant, in practice, that the colonial government did little more than maintain law and order and raise taxes to pay for the cost of the civil establishment and necessary public works. In general, during this period of the empire, colonies were founded to secure commerce and protect the merchant, and to insure such conditions as were necessary for commerce to flourish, for example, the suppression of disorder and the settlement of commercial disputes.[3] From the very outset, the Colonial Office also sought to protect the Chinese. The initial intention was to place the Chinese subjects of Hong Kong under their own Chinese law administered by Chinese officials, but ultimately they were brought under the control of British courts. Still, throughout the ninteenth century, the Colonial Office strove to protect the Chinese from exploitation at the hands of the Europeans in Hong Kong.

The question of representation for the resident European community in Hong Kong was raised early in its history. Sir John Bowring, upon his arrival as governor in April 1854, expressed zeal to reform the Legislative Council by providing for representation. Bowring claimed that his object was to get a popular element in the Legislative Council to represent public opinion and its demands for improvements and social reform in the life of the colony. Bowring also sought free discretion in the allocation and control of funds provided the colony by parliamentary grant through the secretary of state.

---

[2] Ibid., p. 20.

[3] Law and order and contract enforcement are two of the basic tasks undertaken by most governments. Moreover, excepting externalities and public goods, these are perhaps the only tasks, in addition to defense, that governments should undertake to provide.

Bowring's plan for the infusion of an elected element into the council was rejected, because of the peculiar position of Hong Kong. Labouchere, then secretary of state for the colonies, informed Bowring that the island was held not because of its "own advantages" but to serve the commercial interests of trade between the Chinese and British empires. This trade, and the general progress of civilization in the Far East, was predicated upon the maintenance of British rule and orderly government in Hong Kong. Internal insecurity, lawlessness, and proximity to China precluded viable representative government. Labouchere also insisted that Hong Kong's affairs should be conducted with the greatest regard to the feelings and interests of the Chinese population and, accordingly, Chinese might be considered for administrative posts. But an elected Legislative Council was out of the question: "If the Imperial Government had rejected elections, it was not because it objected to governing in accordance with the wishes of the community, but for the very opposite reason, that elections would have given power to a privileged minority which might not have reflected the views of the inhabitants as a whole." [4]

It became common practice early in the history of Hong Kong for well-established members of the merchant community to petition the Colonial Office. Protesting the levying of rates by the governor, the merchants repeatedly demanded some form of local self-government, ostensibly to prevent taxation without representation. Replying to one such request for local government, Sir James Stephen at the Colonial Office caustically wrote: "(i) the English minority can hardly be trusted with the powers which it would give them over Chinese and other alien and ignorant ratepayers; (ii) its existence would probably be incompatible with that decisiveness and energy of proceeding which are almost necessary for the very existence of a European government surrounded by millions of Asiatics." [5] Thus very early in Hong Kong's history the doctrine was recognized that the fate of the native inhabitants must not be entrusted to a comparatively few British residents.

The Chinese, in turn, received substantial benefit from British rule in Hong Kong. Chinese-owned shipping received protection under a local ordinance that allowed Chinese holders of Crown lands in Hong Kong to register their ships on the colony register of shipping and

---

[4] Endacott, *Government and People in Hong Kong,* p. 60.
[5] Quoted in ibid., pp. 75–76.

thereby secure the protection of the British flag. The Chinese also benefited from the stability of the colony's economic life and of its currency, and from the absence of irritating restrictions then so prevalent in China.

The merchant community continued to petition the secretary of state for constitutional reform—greater local control—referring to the municipal governments in the British Crown Colonies of Ceylon and the Straits Settlements. A lengthy reply to one of these petitions was drafted by Lord Ripon, secretary of state for the colonies. He pointed out that Hong Kong was not suited to any form of self-government because it was an imperial station with imperial interests, situated on the borders of a foreign land. Rejecting what he saw as potential control by a small oligarchy of some 800 local merchants, he insisted that the well-being of the large majority of inhabitants, the Chinese, was more likely to be safeguarded by the Colonial Office, through its appointed officials in Hong Kong, than by a system of representation which would leave the bulk of the population wholly unrepresented.[6]

The merchant community in Hong Kong had been seeking a council similar to the one in Shanghai, which denied representation to the Chinese. But Lord Ripon was well aware that the merchants did not seek full representative government which would have handed the colony over to the Chinese. "They wanted an oligarchy of 800 voters and defended this illiberal proposal by appealing to liberal arguments which lost their force by its racial exclusiveness." [7] Lord Ripon's reply to the 1894 petition was supported by his successor, Joseph Chamberlain. Continuity of Colonial Office policy suggested that the two major British political parties agreed that greater political autonomy for Hong Kong's British residents was incompatible with the Crown's moral obligation to protect the interests of the Chinese inhabitants. The Colonial Office maintained that Hong Kong's existing government answered most of the colony's essential needs; it provided the necessary minimum framework of control within which the different communities, each pursuing its own self-interest, could work and live together peacefully. Although Hong Kong was ultimately granted some measure of representation in the appointment of unofficial members to the Legislative

---

[6] See G. B. Endacott, ed., *An Eastern Entrepôt: A Collection of Documents Illustrating the History of Hong Kong* (London: Her Majesty's Stationery Office, 1964), pp. 274–84.

[7] Endacott, *Government and People in Hong Kong,* p. 123.

Council (these being drawn today from the leading elements of the Chinese and European business communities), European merchants were never able to restrict, to their own advantage, the trading activities of Chinese merchants. Trade restrictions would have been inconsistent with the nineteenth century liberal economic doctrine of laissez-faire that knew no color distinctions.[8]

The Philosophy of Government in Hong Kong

The philosophy that underlies government in Hong Kong can be summed up in a few short phrases: law and order, minimum interference in private affairs, and the creation of an environment conducive to profitable investment. Although government performs several economic roles, its departures from a laissez-faire style of economic management are still more the exception than the rule. The state is the ground landlord in Hong Kong and spends about 15 percent of the national income providing roads and water supplies, plus housing for a very high proportion of the working population. Revenues must, therefore, be sufficient to cover the cost of recurrent expenditures and such new public works as roads, water and housing of the labor force, which are essential to maintaining an expanding economy. However, tax rates must be kept down to satisfy members of the business community in the colony, who believe that low taxes are essential in maintaining a high rate of investment. Thus the need to sustain an aura of business confidence insures that the government will adhere, in general, to the practice and ideology of laissez-faire.

Who Runs Hong Kong?

An outline of the main provisions of Hong Kong's constitution can be found in the works of a number of constitutional specialists.[9] For our purposes, it is sufficient to highlight the major features and relate them to the decision-making process.

To begin with, Hong Kong is not a democracy. Administrative and executive authority lies in the hands of appointed civil servants. At the

---

[8] For a somewhat unique view of imperialism, see Roberts and Rabushka, "A Diagrammatic Exposition of an Economic Theory of Imperialism."

[9] See John Rear, "The Law of the Constitution," in Hopkins, ed., *Hong Kong: The Industrial Colony,* pp. 339–415; Endacott, *Government and People in Hong Kong,* pp. 210–28; and *Annual Report, 1971,* pp. 234–47.

higher levels, its personnel have been recruited chiefly from the United Kingdom. As of 1 January 1969, only 71 of the 326 super-scale posts (the most senior positions) were held by locally recruited staff, though this ratio will most likely rise in the future. More important, only two government departments out of nearly 40 in 1969 had Chinese heads. Hence, virtually all legal power in Hong Kong is in the hands of public servants who do not originate in Hong Kong. In the words of Professor Peter Harris, Hong Kong is an "administrative, no-party state." [10]

The office of governor is the central feature of the government in Hong Kong. The governor's powers are defined by the Letters Patent and Royal Instructions of 14 February 1917, with various subsequent amendments through the 1960s. He is, as the representative of the Queen, the head of government and constitutionally accepts his instructions from the secretary of state who is, in turn, responsible to the United Kingdom Parliament. In practice, however, the secretary of state rarely gives instructions to the governor. The governor presides at meetings of the Executive Council, which is his advisory council, whose advice he generally seeks on important policy matters. He is also president of the Legislative Council, where he possesses two votes. All bills passed by the Legislative Council must have his assent before they become law.

The Executive Council consists of five ex officio members—the commander of British forces, the colonial secretary, the attorney general, the secretary for home affairs, and the financial secretary—together with such other persons as are appointed on instructions from the secretary of state. The Legislative Council, consisting of both official and unofficial members, is charged with the responsibility of enacting legislation and controlling the expenditure of public funds. Thus local Hong Kong residents who sit on the Executive and Legislative Councils do so by virtue of appointment, and not as a result of popular elections. These "unofficial members" may have some influence on policy, but they do not normally determine policy. The constitution permits the governor to ignore the advice of his Executive Council, while his two votes as president of the Legislative Council, when combined with the twelve votes of the official members who must always support him on every vote or resign, means that no official government measure may

---

[10] Peter B. Harris, "Political Science and Political Style: Europe, Africa, and Asia (An Inaugural Lecture)," University of Hong Kong, *Supplement to the Gazette,* vol. 18, no. 3 (February 1971), p. 12.

be voted down in that assembly of 25 councilors. Moreover, the Crown can, if it wishes, disallow any ordinance of the Legislative Council through the secretary of state. In any case, those familiar with the style of debate in and the manner of appointment to the Legislative Council know that opposition to government measures is rarely publicly voiced. When political debate does take place, it is usually behind closed doors. The data that a political scientist would find most valuable in practicing his profession in Hong Kong are invariably locked away in files stamped CONFIDENTIAL. *Hansard,* the verbatim report on proceedings in the Legislative Council, does not reveal who makes decisions in Hong Kong nor how they are made.

The following is presented as a theory of decision making in Hong Kong, or in more popular terminology as an answer to the question, Who runs Hong Kong? Recall that the "administrative, no-party state" of Hong Kong does not have an electorate (other than for the relatively unimportant Urban Council, which bears administrative responsibility for such minor tasks as sanitation, running of markets, management of public libraries and government car parks, and maintenance of places for public recreation). Thus, popular expression of preference in the form of periodic elections does not constrain the concentrated power of the bureaucrats. These officials govern under self-imposed limits of power beyond which they feel their actions might incite violent upheaval that would, in turn, scare away investment capital and damage a climate of business confidence. But bureaucrats without resources are powerless. The adage that "he who pays the piper calls the tune" applies just as fully to Hong Kong, where appropriation measures must be approved by the Legislative Council, as it does to the Western democracies wherein parliamentary approval of budgetary requests precedes bureaucratic expenditure.

Standing orders provide for only one standing committee of the Legislative Council—the Finance Committee—which is of the utmost importance within the machinery of government. The unofficial members comprise a majority, meetings are held in private and its proceedings are not published. The only official members who sit on the committee are the colonial secretary (the chairman), the financial secretary, and the director of public works. All proposals involving the expenditure of public funds routinely go to the committee—almost no proposal involving an expenditure of public funds is put to the full meeting of the Legislative Council which has not already been approved by the

Finance Committee. Since most legislation and most executive acts involve the expenditure of funds, this means that the Finance Committee rules on all aspects of government expenditure policy, specifically each government department's annual budget request. Unofficial members may freely speak their minds during these private sessions, thereby preventing open clashes during the public sessions of the Legislative Council, but the privacy of these meetings insures that the extent of influence of the unofficial members in determining public policy remains unknown.

The power of the Finance Committee was considerably enhanced in 1958 with the granting to the colony of a wide measure of financial autonomy. This was announced by the governor, Sir Robert Black, in the course of his annual address to the Legislative Council on 6 March 1958:

> Before concluding, I have to report a decision recently taken by the Secretary of State. He has approved a considerable relaxation in the financial control which he exercises over Hong Kong. In 1948 the Colony was released from Treasury control and given a large measure of autonomy over its own finances. The control which the Secretary of State still retained at that time was that his approval was still required for the annual Estimates, for supplementary provisions exceeding $1 million in the case of capital expenditure, and for the issue of any loan and for any expenditure involving important points of principle. The Secretary of State has now informed me that, in view of the good standing, financial and administrative, of the Colony, he will further relax his control and will no longer require the Estimates to be submitted for his approval; nor will he require supplementary provisions to be authorized by him.[11]

Since this measure reserved the control of the secretary of state only for the raising of loans and for financial matters involving important points of principle, the 1958 enactment can be considered the most significant constitutional development introduced into postwar Hong Kong. These provisions broadened the 1948 constitutional arrangement and transferred financial powers to the colony's Legislative Council, which, as we have seen, considers financial matters only after the prior approval of the Finance Committee.

Retention of business confidence suggests, however, that govern-

[11] Quoted in Endacott, *Government and People in Hong Kong,* pp. 200–201.

ment would first consult leading members of the community before undertaking controversial legislation. Analysts of Hong Kong often suggest monolithic, power-elite views of political control:

> A number of writers have expressed the view that Hong Kong is actually controlled by about 20 persons, and while this could be criticized as extreme—and certainly impossible to prove—it could just as well be said that it is controlled by not more than ten persons: the governor; the colonial secretary; the financial secretary; the director of public works; managing director of Jardine, Matheson & Co. (the most powerful and longest-established business house); the general manager of the Hongkong & Shanghai Bank (the leading financial institution); the two most influential Chinese members of the Executive and Legislative Councils; and the most prominent Portuguese and Indian member of the Executive or Legislative Council. Perhaps the best way to test this top-ten theory would be to try running something in opposition to these ten, and no one has ventured that yet.[12]

John Rear outlines a somewhat different version of the alliance between the British business community and government, the former having both a nationalistic and financial interest in the preservation of the colonial system:

> The power bloc formed by such organizations, to name a few of the apparent leaders, as the Hongkong and Shanghai Banking Corporation, Hutchison International Ltd., Jardine, Matheson & Co., Ltd., Butterfield & Swire (H.K.) Ltd., the Dairy Farm, Ice & Cold Storage Co., Ltd., Wheelock Marden & Co., Ltd., who between them own a vast network of subsidiary companies, must obviously be influential. This bloc is certainly very strongly represented in Legislative and Executive Councils. . . . The Colony's small size facilitates continual social and business contacts between the leaders of Government and the business community. . . . The over-all impression left is that the main stream of influence on the Hong Kong Government comes from a relatively narrow circle in which there are no basic differences in outlook and certainly no clash of ideologies.[13]

Although one would be foolish to deny the influence of business in public policy formulation, the above widely held views probably ascribe

[12] Gleason, *Hong Kong,* pp. 214–15.
[13] Rear, "One Brand of Politics," pp. 79–80.

more power to leading business elements than is really the case. Reading the proceedings of the Legislative Council reveals that in the area of financial policy the unofficial members—this monolithic mercantile community—come up against the obstacle of the financial secretary's rigid adherence to his own axioms of policy. Note first a speech by Y. K. Kan in the Legislative Council meeting of 11 March 1965 in which he complained that the Finance Committee of the Legislative Council and its two subcommittees, the establishment and public works subcommittees, only see items for approval if they are accepted by the colonial secretariat. "What is not accepted seldom, if ever, goes any further." [14] Kan's speech, in effect, affirmed that the Finance Committee and its parent body, the Legislative Council, do not enjoy the opportunity to put to the vote what the financial secretary and colonial secretary have determined not to place on the agenda.

The answer to Kan's complaint by the colonial secretary during the meeting of 26 March 1965 indicates government's attitude. The colonial secretary replied that proposals marshaled and presented by the secretariat follow the same procedures as practiced in Britain by the Treasury. To submit proposals directly to the Finance Committee without further official scrutiny or support would lead to considerable confusion and reduce the constitutional power of government.[15]

At a Legislative Council meeting of 7 October 1970 Y. K. Kan again expressed his desire that the Finance Committee should open its proceedings by sitting in public to allow members of the local community to better understand its workings and discussions. "These committees sit in private; consequently their work is hidden from the public eye." [16] The colonial secretary's reply pointed to the great volume of business conducted in the Finance Committee. If it operated under the public eye, he said, it would be likely to lose a great deal of its efficiency.[17]

Perhaps the real power of the so-called local business elite is revealed by K. S. Lo's speech during a February 1971 meeting of the Legislative Council. This unofficial member suggested that he and his colleagues should be empowered to introduce financial measures into Legislative Council meetings. He claimed that *"It is only the Financial Secretary*

---

[14] *Hong Kong Hansard 1965.*
[15] Ibid.
[16] *Hong Kong Hansard 1970.*
[17] Ibid.

who can initiate proposals for financial expenditures and he determines the priorities of projects. What comes before the Finance Committee has been *carefully vetted by him and the Finance Branch* and unofficial members have only the negative power to refuse to approve an expenditure." [18]

The director of public works is clearly subordinate to the financial secretary in Hong Kong's administrative hierarchy—rarely does he retire with the knighthood that is bestowed upon a successful financial secretary. Thus power resides in the hands of the colonial secretary, the financial secretary, and the governor. But the governor is usually dependent on the financial secretary for economic and financial decisions. The colonial secretary is kept busy advising the governor on matters not purely financial or economic, and acts for him in his absence. This, therefore, singles out the financial secretary as the man who runs Hong Kong, that is, the man with the power of the purse, at least during the postwar period until mid-1971. This conclusion is affirmed by John Rear, who states that Sir John Cowperthwaite, financial secretary from 1962 to 1971, was generally regarded as the dominant figure in the government.[19] Interviews with heads of government departments and other knowledgeable informants corroborate this view. The *Far Eastern Economic Review* of 10 October 1970, commenting on Cowperthwaite's impending retirement, noted that he was a man generally aloof, but that his period of rule had been very good for growth. If this theory of decision making in Hong Kong is correct, then much of Hong Kong's remarkable record of postwar economic growth, especially during the last decade, can be attributed to the extremely wise rule of the Scottish financial secretary, specifically to the practice of his generally laissez-faire policy. Haddon-Cave's appointment as the new financial secretary in mid-1971 foreshadows some possible new departures in policy, and their implications are explored in the final chapter.

As mentioned in Chapter 3, external forces may be more important for the Hong Kong economy than purely domestic considerations. The financial secretary, therefore, is not in a position where he can create real wealth or value, but only in a position to influence conditions within the colony that might be conducive to high productivity, lucrative investment, and maintaining the prevalence of the profit motive. The rais-

[18] *South China Morning Post,* February 13, 1971.
[19] Rear, "One Brand of Politics," p. 65.

ing of taxes, collection of statistics, expansion of the civil service, welfare services, et cetera, are just some of the things under his influence, and hence, the man who occupies the office of the financial secretary can play a critical role. The attractiveness of Hong Kong to date is found in its fundamentally laissez-faire outlook, low taxes, and absence of counterproductive regulations—features which distinguish Hong Kong from some of its corrupt, incompetent Southeast Asian neighbors. It is the burden of the financial secretary to insure this continued distinction by maintaining an attractive environment for investment.

The Economics of Government

The Hong Kong government, in some ways, appears to operate more like the classical notion of the business firm than the contemporary welfare notion of the state in which government seeks to correct market failures and provide public goods. Surplus of revenue over expenditure for the 1971-1972 fiscal year reveals a rate of return to operating expense of more than 20 percent, a rate higher than that earned by many private firms (see Table 6). Hong Kong's fiscal policy is not the result of chance, but lies in the conscious decisions of the financial secretary. Hong Kong's record of fiscal responsibility stands in a favorable light when compared with the irresponsible inflationary practice of most contemporary governments.

Why do the books of the Hong Kong government show an annual surplus? The most popular explanation asserts that as Hong Kong is a colony, it must be of benefit to the mother country. To prove this assertion is nearly impossible. But the colony does maintain huge reserves in the United Kingdom which are equivalent to between one-quarter and one-third of Britain's total gold and foreign exchange reserves.[20] The sterling backing for the expanding issue of Hong Kong dollars and the long- and short-term sterling securities purchased with surplus government revenues each year are considerable. The Statement of Assets and Liabilities of 31 March 1971 lists about HK$220 million in sterling fixed deposits and HK$911 million in sterling investments.[21] Since Britain's reserves are often quickly depleted given her historical experiences with balance-of-payments deficits, the maintenance of Hong

---

[20] Ibid., p. 59.

[21] *Annual Report, 1971,* p. 275.

Kong's reserve assets in sterling constitutes an external source of support for the pound that would, if significantly diversified into other currencies, further weaken the pound in Britain's overall trading and balance-of-payments accounts.

The Hong Kong government follows a fiscal policy intended to avoid deficits. Table 9 compares the actual surplus or deficit for each fiscal year against the estimated surplus/deficit. Only once, for fiscal year 1965-66, did the deficit actually exceed the estimate. In all other postwar years, estimated surpluses have been grossly understated and most estimated deficits disappeared altogether in the face of buoyant revenue. Some scholars argue that government deliberately underestimates revenue and overestimates expenditures, and thus there is considerable margin for the expansion of, say, welfare services. If these surpluses are indeed planned, this policy has accumulated reserves that would permit sustained government expenditure over a long recession without serious cutbacks. If the surpluses are unplanned, then they are largely due to conservative fiscal policy. In the absence of government borrowing, reserves provide the sole means of financing a deficit. The cumulative surplus as of April 1972 was equal to approximately HK$2,800 million, or about 100 percent of the 1971-1972 authorized expenditure.[22]

Table 9 indicates that the only serious deficit in postwar Hong Kong occurred during fiscal year 1965-66. Was it purely coincidence that the rate of tax on earnings and profits was raised in 1966 from 12½ to 15 percent? Probably not. The rise converted a large projected deficit for 1966-1967 to a small surplus and has since contributed to ever-growing surpluses. (In keeping with Hong Kong's basically laissez-faire policy, it is somewhat surprising that the tax rate was not lowered after 1968 to its earlier level of 12½ or even 10 percent.)

A notable characteristic of Hong Kong public finance is that there is almost a complete absence of public debt. The public debt of the colony at 31 March 1971 stood at $60.4 million, or $15 per capita.[23] This low level is especially remarkable since the Hong Kong government pays for its prodigious public works program, particularly the colony's water works and urban housing projects, out of current revenue. The accumulation of large surpluses in the varying economic conditions which Hong Kong has experienced since the war is extremely

---

22 *Hong Kong Monthly Digest of Statistics,* April 1972, Table 8.6.
23 *Annual Report, 1971,* p. 278.

Table 9
ACTUAL SURPLUS/DEFICIT COMPARED WITH ESTIMATED SURPLUS/DEFICIT
(HK$ millions)

Year	Actual Surplus (+) Deficit (−)	Estimated Surplus (+) Deficit (−)
1946-47	−3.5	−116.5
1947-48	+36.6	0.0
1948-49	+35.0	+1.1
1949-50	+82.1	+0.2
1950-51	+40.0	+3.3
1951-52	+32.7	+13.1
1952-53	+72.8	+2.1
1953-54	+41.5	+20.5
1954-55	+61.1	+1.2
1955-56	+52.3	−35.4
1956-57	+40.1	−43.3
1957-58	+51.5	−53.7
1958-59	+39.4	−94.1
1959-60	−45.3	−92.4
1960-61	+13.9	−226.1
1961-62	+77.2	−160.9
1962-63	+139.8	−163.9
1963-64	+98.5	−163.0
1964-65	+77.8	−114.3
1965-66	−137.4	−60.0
1966-67	+11.7	−94.1
1967-68	+133.5	−37.0
1968-69	+208.1	−13.0
1969-70	+448.5	+53.4
1970-71	+618.7	+191.1
1971-72	+602.0	+256.0

Source: *Hong Kong Statistics, 1947-1967,* Table 9.11 and *Hong Kong Annual Reports,* 1947-1971.

impressive and indicative of fiscal integrity. Moreover, it has taken place after charging annually against current revenue all capital expenditure other than a comparatively small amount financed by borrowing. These annual capital spendings have been as high as $735 million; in 1970-71 they totaled some $551 million. Public expenditures for water works and roads in the 1970s may require even higher sums.

Why have revenues increased so much more rapidly than expenditures, and at a rate exceeding government's official published estimates? The government reply is that:

Table 10
CUMULATIVE GOVERNMENT SURPLUS
(HK$ millions)

Fiscal Year (March 31st)	**Cumulative Official Surplus**	**Revenue Equalization Fund**
1947-48	37.0	—
1948-49	72.1	—
1949-50	154.1	—
1950-51	192.9	—
1951-52	222.0	—
1952-53	196.9	100.0[a]
1953-54	242.4	137.4
1954-55	293.8	137.5
1955-56	311.4	137.6
1956-57	358.2	137.7
1957-58	401.5	137.8
1958-59	461.0	137.9
1959-60	406.7	138.0
1960-61	n.a.	138.0
1961-62	493.4	138.0
1962-63	659.1	138.0
1963-64	761.7	138.0
1964-65	822.9	138.0
1965-66	687.9	138.0
1966-67	710.2	138.0
1967-68	787.6	138.0
1968-69	949.3	138.0
1969-70	1,633.2	138.0
1970-71	2,284.5	138.0
1971-72	2,886.0	138.0

[a] Instituted in 1953.
Source: Calculated from *Hong Kong Annual Reports,* 1948-1971 and *Hong Kong Monthly Digest of Statistics,* April 1972, Table 8.6.

The principal reason for these results . . . was that during the earlier years exceptionally rapid increases in population generated economic activity which raised the yield from taxation and other sources of revenue without appreciable increases in the rates of tax. Revenue expanded from $292 million in 1950-51 to $3,071 million in 1970-71. The rate of increase was affected by variations in such factors as the economic situation and inflows of capital, but the upward trend has been strong and continuous. In expenditure there was inevitably a time-lag before the government could develop

> the public and social services necessary for an increasing population and made possible by economic growth itself.[24]

Apart from the need to maintain reserves pending future deficits, why didn't the government announce a tax refund or lower the tax rates?

Critics use the huge government reserves to recommend increases in welfare expenditures. But in fairness to the Hong Kong government, the record of welfare programs in the West attests that it is one thing to appropriate public revenues and quite another to spend them effectively. Money spent unwisely frequently does more harm than good. Furthermore, repeated budget surpluses do more for maintaining business confidence than do sustained deficits.

The Hong Kong government directly provides a number of economic services and regulates still other functions for which the classic laissez-faire notion does not provide. Some of these services are land reclamation, water works, and massive urban housing projects. Two questions are, therefore, immediately raised. First, why does the Hong Kong government perform these economic services? Secondly, how does government manage its economic affairs?

The water works are probably the most readily agreed-upon necessary task of government. It is alleged that no consortium of private investors would provide sufficient capital, and also that private citizens should not be entrusted with its management in view of the peculiar political geography of Hong Kong and the political delicacies involved when water must be rationed. But the forecast expenditure of $2,000 million on water works by 1975-76 is well within the means of local entrepreneurs, and the essentially private operation of transport, electricity, harbor, and telephone services suggests that the second reason is also not convincing. Some officials argue that water is more crucial for human survival and hence more politically delicate than the provision of transport, electricity, or telephone services. But Hong Kong's dynamic economy would soon collapse in the absence of transport, electricity or telephone services, all of which are privately owned and operated for private profit. Since Hong Kong's increased use of power has been aided by the steadily diminishing prices charged by a private firm, the argument that government must supply water is not altogether persuasive, although large-scale land acquisition might complicate efforts

[24] Ibid., p. 43.

at private provision. Profit maximization applies equally to water supply as to power generation.

Though run by government, the water works program is, like many publicly supplied services, self-supporting. Reflecting this management view, water charges were increased in 1965 and then again in 1971 to bring revenues in line with costs and to acquire funds to support future water works developments.

Roads and town planning seem less controversial since it is difficult to establish an efficient system of user-charges for roads—thus a case can be made that government rightly should undertake their building and maintenance. It is not immediately apparent, however, why government should dominate reclamation and heavily regulate the sale of land, save the resale of existing Crown leases. A full understanding of this practice requires some historical background.

In a series of letters and instruments, all dated 4 January 1843, addressed by Lord Aberdeen to Sir Henry Pottinger, Hong Kong's first governor, a number of temporary measures for the administration of Hong Kong were set forth. Among the governor's duties he was to make grants of land, except

> that H. M. Government would not choose that . . . grants should be made to parties whose object in obtaining such grants would be to dispose of them again with advantage to themselves. . . . He was further told that if, as a result of the establishment of a free port and the introduction of those liberal arrangements by which foreigners would be encouraged to come, a great commercial entrepôt were created, then H. M. Government would feel justified in securing to the Crown the increased values that the land would then have.[25]

All land in Hong Kong is thus owned by the Crown. Except in the New Territories, which must be handed over to China in 1997, all Crown leases are granted for 75 years, usually renewable for a further 75 years at a reassessed Crown rent. Basic policy is to sell leases to the highest bidder at public auction. This includes all land available to the general public for commercial and industrial purposes and for residential sites.

Land sales totaled under $10 million annually before 1954, increased in steps to about $90 million in 1961, and a building boom

[25] Quoted in Endacott, *Government and People in Hong Kong*, pp. 20–21.

between 1962 and 1965 earned over $100 million in revenue each year. Sales fell below $50 million annually between the 1966-67 and 1968-69 fiscal years, but have since risen to $120 million in 1969-70 and $271 million for 1970-71.

Although government owns and allocates all the land in Hong Kong, it places heavy reliance on the market mechanism. Industrial land is scarce in Hong Kong and must be rationed efficiently to ensure that each square foot generates the maximum income for the colony. Firms that are able to pay high rents to obtain space are precisely the ones that can generate these high incomes. Historical circumstance and considerable revenue from land sales, then, seem to account for public ownership of land, in place of a fully defined set of private property rights that would appear to be more consistent with a free economy.

Not only does government hold title to all the colony's land, it is landlord to more than 40 percent of the colony's residents as well. In 1953, in order to cope with the housing shortage created by an influx of refugees from China, the government began a crash building program. For squatters who illegally occupied land required for development, accommodation known as resettlement estates was built. Many persons housed in resettlement estates had been compulsorily evicted from squatter housing. These estates have produced high-density communities, designed to provide 24 square feet of living space per adult family member. As of 1971, 25 resettlement estates housed 1,147,860 persons. For residents of overcrowded tenements with a maximum income of HK$1,000 per month, the government had built by 1971 nine housing authority estates which accommodate 218,450 persons. Finally, for persons with maximum monthly incomes of HK$500, the government manages 15 low-cost housing estates that shelter 258,373 residents. Including housing for public employees, the Hong Kong government is landlord to about 44 percent of the population, surely the most extensive public housing scheme ever completed anywhere! [26]

Why has the government engaged in this socialized housing scheme? In part, the reason is due to limited land and the inability or unwillingness of the private sector to provide adequate low-rent housing since competing forms of investment have normally offered higher rates

---

[26] *Annual Report, 1971,* p. 18. For an interesting treatment of the housing problem in Hong Kong, see Keith Hopkins, "Housing the Poor," in Hopkins, ed., *Hong Kong: The Industrial Colony,* pp. 271–335.

of return to capital. Additionally, these programs may have had an initially unintended effect of keeping the economy buoyant by housing a large labor force which thus stimulated private enterprise, in turn keeping government revenues buoyant.

Rents in government housing are exceptionally low. Rents in all public housing in Hong Kong in 1969 averaged less than 10 percent (6 percent in resettlement estates) of median household incomes. Moreover, this low rate of rent in public housing has remained fairly constant since 1954, when those evicted from squatter housing had to be resettled inexpensively. Tenants in the private sector typically pay much more rent, often with less space and inferior amenities. From a market point of view, rents in the public sector could be raised to yield more revenue without causing hardship, thereby providing funds to build more and better housing. Low rents discourage movement out of public housing into the private sector and encourage overcrowding. Hopkins claims that rents have remained low partly because of the ignorance of the actual earnings of squatters and partly to avoid trouble.[27] To raise the rents to their current market value would, he believes, probably create the kind of upheaval or dissent that the colonial government wishes to avoid. Those government officials in favor of low rents are probably more interested in contented tenants than orthodox finance. There are also hints that some housing officials profit handsomely from the authority to allocate below market price accommodation, wherein excess demand entails some arbitrary rationing criteria. Incentives for raising rents in public housing may not, therefore, be compelling for these administrators and their tenants.

Yet another departure from laissez-faire is found in the various rent control ordinances of government. Legislation controlling rents and providing security of tenure was instituted by proclamation immediately after World War II and embodied in 1947 in the Landlord and Tenant Ordinance. It applied to both domestic and business premises and restricted rents by reference to prewar levels, while excluding new and substantially reconstructed buildings from control. A maximum rise from the prewar level of 30 percent in domestic and 45 percent in business premises was allowed. Following an amendment in 1953, increases in standard rents were permitted to 55 percent above prewar

---

27 Hopkins, "Housing the Poor," p. 299.

levels for domestic and 150 percent for business premises, where they have remained ever since.

The origins of rent control may be protectionist—they obviously contradict the maxim of laissez-faire which implies the landlord's right to collect in rent the full market value of his premises. Rent controls were designed to protect the tenant. Many long-time residents in Hong Kong would otherwise have been displaced by immigrants with the resources to pay higher rents. And as noted before government intervenes in the allocation of land for industrial purposes to reserve certain coastal sites for such industries as electricity generation and boat building. Altogether, then, government's role as landowner, landlord, and regulator of premises constitutes a departure from the ideology and practice of laissez-faire, though perhaps occasioned by the peculiar circumstances found in Hong Kong: colonial status, land and water shortages and uncontrollable increases in population.

Responsibility for the operation of Hong Kong's airport and supervision of all aspects of civil aviation in the colony rest with the Civil Aviation Department. A first explanation is the existence of international obligations and restrictions on use in the provision and control of international airports. A second answer can be found in the colony's statement of public debt. In addition to a rehabilitation loan granted in 1947-48, the colony's only other outstanding debt is the Kai Tak Airport development loan. This *interest-free* loan of 3 million pounds, granted in 1961 by the United Kingdom for the development of Hong Kong's airport, was made when airport expansion was deemed vital to preserve for Hong Kong a key stop on international air routes, at a time when, perhaps, the private sector would have been unable to finance this expansion. Revenue from the operation of Kai Tak was first published as a separate item in the *1964 Annual Report* and only for the 1964-1965 estimate. Hence the cost or benefits of government-managed airport operations prior to 1965 cannot be evaluated. Revenue obtained from airport operations in fiscal 1970-1971 exceeded $81 million; at the same time expenditure on the Civil Aviation Department was just under $13 million.[28] If these two budget categories fully disclose all costs and benefits in airport operations, then government management of Kai Tak is indeed efficient. Nearly 1¼ million departing passengers paid a required HK$10 fee, in addition to various landing

[28] *Annual Report, 1971,* pp. 271–73.

and other charges that were collected. Historical factors and international practices thus explain why management of the airport rests with government. However, a new freight terminal is intended to be privately financed and managed.

The government also directly operates the British section of the Kowloon-Canton Railway which runs from the Tsim Sha Tsui station to Lo Wu on the Chinese railway system. It is government owned and run for both historical and financial reasons. It was financed in 1910-11 by what was then a colossal public loan of HK$15 million for its construction. It was originally built as a freight link with China but has now become a suburban railway. An analysis of revenues and expenditures reveals the railway to be extremely well managed. Revenue for fiscal 1970-1971 totaled HK$15.9 million; expenditures were just under HK$10.8 million.[29] This represents a rate of return to operating expense of nearly 50 percent. Excepting a deficit for fiscal 1962-1963, government has obtained a net surplus on railway operations each year of no less than HK$3 million since 1963 and has usually averaged between HK$5 and $7 million.[30]

Over the past decade, the railway has earned approximately $45 million for the Hong Kong treasury. In recent years competition in the form of bus, taxi, and pirate taxi services has helped determine the railroad price. Public housing, on the other hand, does not face competition from the private sector.

Government's management style is clearly governed by the philosophy of self-support and it seeks to operate any economic service on a commercial basis. A budget deficit in 1965-1966 encouraged a tax rise; losses in the water works stimulated two recent hikes in water charges; the airport and railway, on a percentage basis, number among Hong Kong's most profitable enterprises, both public and private. But the government also provides a number of services that are visibly uneconomic, that is, they lose money—these services seem motivated by genuine humanitarian concern. For example, government has generally provided low-cost or free medical services for those unable to afford private treatment. Any person may attend a government clinic on payment of a nominal fee of $1, which includes drug charges. Those admitted to the public wards of a government hospital pay a maximum

29 Ibid.

30 *Annual Reports,* 1963–71.

daily fee of $2, which is often waived for hardship cases. These medical services are paid for out of general revenue. In fiscal 1970-1971 the Medical and Health Department spent over $177 million of which clinic fees contributed only a small portion.

The government subsidy to education approached $400 million in fiscal 1970-1971, a dramatic rise over the past few years. An additional appropriation of $93 million was authorized for Hong Kong's two universities, but the majority of funds still go into primary education. Until 1971, education was not fully subsidized in Hong Kong and parents of pupils had to pay school fees and pay for textbooks and school activities, although poor families received substantial subsidies. Between 1948 and 1968, government increased its expenditure on education 20 times; school enrollment correspondingly grew ninefold. Market forces have historically played a large role in the provision of education, tempered with public support for the less affluent. A new educational policy, discussed in the final chapter, represents a major departure from government's reliance on market forces and public expenditure on education can be expected to rise rapidly over the next few years.

The government also underwrites Radio Hong Kong, a government station, which is financed from general revenue and carries no advertising. This station features information and public affairs in contrast to Commercial Radio, which operates as a private firm deriving revenues from advertising. The existence of a government radio network is probably due to the government wanting to have one medium of communication with the people in its own hands.

Through the Urban Council, the government operates six multistory parking garages with a total capacity of 3,599 cars; a seventh is due for completion in 1972. Though the financial secretary announced his intent to raise parking charges in the 1972 budget speech, the fees are still too low as the long queue of cars outside each lot attests. Government's unwillingness to charge for the full market value of a parking space may be attributable to the fact that the motorist is articulate and well able to voice his protest over rising parking charges; it may also be government's unofficial policy to subsidize the private motorist. Admittedly, it is difficult to determine whether the ambivalent nature of the tax he pays on fuel is payment for facilities or a tax on consumption.

Thus far we have examined a number of economic services that government directly provides. Some of these produce a handsome surplus while others are direct subsidies for perhaps humanitarian or political reasons. But government's economic role is not limited just to those services it directly provides; parts of the private sector are closely regulated as well. These include such basic fields as banking, the rice trade, fish marketing, power generation, housing, and public transport. The government has also taken a 25 percent share in the cost and operation of the cross-harbor tunnel.

The increased regulation of banks, though motivated by a banking crisis in 1965 and enacted to protect the depositor, effectively benefits the existing banks already established in Hong Kong by protecting them from increased competition. Since 1965, all new applications for bank licenses but one have been refused. Cowperthwaite readily admits that "it was partly because we did not wish to see any new banks incorporated in Hong Kong that we have refused further licenses since then." [31] The only exception that is made at present is to an application from a bank incorporated in one of Hong Kong's export markets and yet unrepresented by a bank in Hong Kong—subject, of course, to the criterion of reciprocity. He insisted, however, that government does not object to foreign banks acquiring a major interest in a Hong Kong bank, though the power to control this also exists. Agitation is presently growing in some quarters in the colony for similar government control of Hong Kong's four stock exchanges, which at the time of this writing are free from government control.

With the exception of the Kowloon-Canton Railway, public transport is operated by private enterprise. There are five major public transport companies operating scheduled services under ordinances which grant monopoly rights but require the provision of adequate services. These are China Motor Bus and Hongkong Tramways which serve Hong Kong Island, Kowloon Motor Bus which has the exclusive franchise in Kowloon and the mainland portion of the New Territories, and Hongkong and Yaumati Ferry and Star Ferry which operate services across the harbor and between the islands.

What do monopoly franchise rights for these five transport firms entail? Under government concessions Hongkong Tramway pays royalties to government at a fixed rate just over 20 percent of its annual net

[31] *The Banker,* July 1970, p. 738.

profits. The fare is, however, fixed by government, which carefully calculates the fair return on the company's capital assets and then sets the appropriate charge. The two bus companies also operate under special franchises that provide for royalty payments to government. Lastly, the two ferry companies pay a varying royalty rate depending on their monthly receipts, in addition to a fixed pier rental.

What problems does government franchise of public transport pose for the private provision of adequate service? Rising costs, for one, cannot be met with a fare increase unless authorized by government. Instead, companies must reduce overhead and operating costs. The bus companies, for example, have either reduced the number of conductors on buses or eliminated them altogether to reduce costs. The government has recently agreed to fare readjustments for the bus firms, and to a revaluation of the capital assets of the tramway company for purposes of determining a fair rate of return on capital assets. It has also authorized the operation of over 3,800 licensed vehicles known as public light buses, which provide additional passenger services on the basis of privately set routes and fares. The fact that public light buses returned somewhere between 100 and 200 percent per year for the value of their investment in their first two years of operation indicates that in the absence of competition, the franchised monopolies were not compelled to supply an adequate, correctly priced service. Declines in revenues of the franchised bus firms, caused by the introduction of the public light buses, indicate that regulation of transport impeded efficient provision of transport services.

Government franchise of transport has served, in effect, to protect existing firms from competition. Overwhelming acceptance by the public of the minibus service introduced in 1968 suggests that full dependence on market forces would supply Hong Kong with more adequate public transportation than the present system of franchised monopolies, the latter having contributed to reduced employment opportunities as a result of the need to cut costs. Taxing the profits of transport companies might have produced revenue for government equal to revenue from the present system of royalty arrangements, which on occasion has been temporarily suspended due to unprofitable operations. Market pressures would seem to insure more efficient private provision of public transport.

The review contained in this chapter gives a fair picture of the economic roles of the Hong Kong government and how they compare with the classical model of laissez-faire which stipulates that government should do no more than enforce contracts and maintain law and order. A complete list of public services is found in the colony's ordinances itemized in the *Annual Reports*. But the basic pattern is clear: Some services produce a surplus, others break even, and still others are subsidized. Other economic activities in the private sector are also closely regulated. The reasons for the choice of one mode of provision over another at times seem historic, sometimes commercial and at other times entirely humanitarian.

5

New Departures in Public Policy

Since the occupation of Hong Kong in 1841, the idea of laissez-faire has influenced government's relationship to the private sector. But practice has departed in some measure from this model of a "hands-off" policy toward the economy—witness the direct provision of several economic services by government and the close regulation of certain fields in the private sector. Some of these policies have been gradual postwar innovations: rent control on prewar premises, successive increments in the earnings and profits tax rates, and increased regulation of banking. Historical and economic interpretations of these policies have been examined as well as the rationale for their continued implementation. Now we will examine several recently authorized government programs which constitute yet an additional shift away from the theory and practice of nonintervention.

It is appropriate to begin with a passage from the introductory review essay in the 1971 *Annual Report*. "The task that lies ahead now is to ensure that the efforts of both the community and the Government are used in the *properly planned* and common objective of raising the social benefits and standards of living for all and of making Hong Kong a better place in which to live."[1] (Italics supplied.) As well, 1971 saw the announcement of a number of new programs that seemed to signify an admitted departure from the free-market model previously acknowledged as the basis of government action.

The first of these went into effect on 1 January 1971: an expanded public assistance scheme, a program Cowperthwaite had advocated

[1] Page 20.

prior to his retirement. The new program entails cash grants in lieu of assistance in kind for persons meeting the eligibility requirements. A single person who has been resident in Hong Kong for more than a year and is beyond the working age of 55, unfit, or not available for work, and has less than HK$70 a month after allowing for rent and essential traveling expenses is, in general, eligible for assistance. Thus HK$70 a month represents a guaranteed level of income. For families, the equivalent level after allowing for rent, school expenses and traveling costs is HK$50 for each of the first three members, HK$40 each for the next three and HK$30 thereafter. When actual income is less than the guaranteed level, the difference is made up by a monthly cash payment.

Has the scheme been successful? Expenditure for public assistance payments in the nine months from 1 April to 31 December 1971 totaled about HK$8.5 million compared with HK$6 million for fiscal 1970-71. The number of public assistance cases at the end of 1971 had risen to 12,533 compared with 7,010 the year before.[2] To cope with this additional administrative burden, the social welfare services expanded from 1,427 posts to 1,519; government expenditure on welfare, a portion of which goes into the public assistance scheme, also increased 27 percent over 1970 to nearly HK$43 million.[3] Although undoubtedly well motivated, government must remain watchful to ensure that these public assistance programs do not get out of hand, as have similar programs in the United States and the United Kingdom. The notion of a free-trading society seems more compatible with private charity than with public assistance.

Another departure from the market for which the government takes pride is its new educational program. Free primary education was introduced in 1971 in all government schools (except the five English language schools) and in the majority of aided primary schools. This was made possible by the fact that there were by then enough places for all, although compulsory primary education had been a goal for many years. In addition, a new post-primary education policy was announced which aims at giving three years of aided education to all children in the 12 to 14 age group; an effort will be made to provide places for 50 percent of them by 1976. The most significant aspect of the 1971 Education Ordinance is that it gives the director of education

[2] *Annual Report, 1971,* pp. 132–33.
[3] Ibid., p. 129.

the power to order parents to send their children to school where it appears to him that they are withholding them from primary school without reasonable excuse—a form of compulsory primary education.[4] Parents who fail to comply could be charged with committing an offense against the law.

The government's belief is that universal, free compulsory primary education means that no child need reasonably be deprived of an opportunity for education. Putting this belief into practice, however, imposes the cost of having the government replace the family elders in evaluating the child's educational needs—a significant infringement on the freedom of the parent. Throughout the history of Hong Kong, the secretary of state for the colonies repeatedly reaffirmed British respect for the cultural practices and freedoms of the resident Chinese community. The 1971 Education Ordinance, taking from the parent the right to choose if his child should attend school, is not in keeping with historical tradition. Most Chinese place a high premium on educating their children and therefore do not strongly object to this measure. Nonetheless, the compulsory provision in the law strikes a contrast with a live-and-let-live tradition, and also works against the immediate financial interests of poor families.

With the implementation in 1971 of the Marriage Reform Ordinance, all marriages hereafter taking place in the colony are restricted to monogamous marriages. This ordinance brings to an end customary marriages, the so-called Chinese modern marriages, and the ancient custom of concubinage,[5] and represents yet another intrusion in the historically defended freedom of the Chinese to practice their own cultural traditions. Despite the fact that this new ordinance mirrors the legal changes that have taken place in China, the cultural life of the Chinese has nonetheless become more circumscribed as a result of this law. This ordinance is an example of a noneconomic regulation by government, but one which still imposes very real, but perhaps not monetary, costs upon the citizenry.

One policy change traceable directly to Cowperthwaite's retirement is found in the new program of data collection in the statistics department. At Haddon-Cave's request, gross national product statistics are now assembled; whether the government will choose to use them in a

[4] Ibid., p. 71.
[5] *Annual Report, 1970,* p. 221.

possible planning role is as yet unknown. Given the existence of these statistics, the possibility of increased planning by government is enhanced. Cowperthwaite's objection to national accounts statistics lay, in part, in his fear that the figures would permit and ultimately foster greater government participation in the economy. Although the new financial secretary may adhere to the tradition of minimal planning, there is no guarantee he can withstand the pressures both within and outside government to use these figures to institute greater government control over the economy. Nor can he control what his successor might do.

Measures in the fields of urban renewal, rent control, labor legislation, and pollution control also point to a growing economic role for government. The 1965 *Report of the Working Party on Slum Clearance* proposed the creation of an urban renewal district, which comprises some 250 acres in the western and Sai Ying Pun districts on Hong Kong Island, and a smaller pilot scheme area in the west central part of the island. Approval was given in 1969 for the planning and engineering feasibility study prepared by the Public Works Department and 90 properties had been acquired by 1971 at a cost of about HK$9 million. Urban renewal has as its purpose government acquisition of sites considered essential to prevent further deterioration of the environment and to provide space for desired community facilities.[6] Two features of urban renewal merit emphasis. First, the law gives government the power of compulsory acquisition which means that owners of "unattractively antiquated buildings" that "lack light and air" will have to sell their properties and may not receive fair market value for them. Second, government participation in urban renewal adds to its growing economic pursuits. The difficulty with public, as opposed to private, urban renewal is that bureaucrats are not forced by the competition to be efficient; also expanding government budgets increase opportunities for bureaucratic corruption. Moreover, if government should retain control after redevelopment, market prices may not prevail which would lead to further inefficiencies in management.

A temporary freeze in rents for postwar domestic premises enacted in January 1970, followed in June by the Rent Increases (Domestic Premises) Control Ordinance 1970, displays the trappings of permanence. Rent controls provide security of tenure for tenants of post-

[6] *Annual Report, 1971,* pp. 19, 171; *Annual Report, 1969,* p. 121.

war domestic premises on flats renting for HK$1,500 per month or less for the life of the ordinance (two years), or for a period of two years from the date of any increase in rent. A number of larger flats and houses, in addition to new lettings, are not controlled.[7] Due to expire on 31 May 1972 this ordinance has been extended for a further two years with an allowable annual rent increase of 5 percent. The mercantile communities are becoming increasingly vocal in their demand for rent controls on business premises; this demand the government has so far successfully resisted.

Rent control for postwar domestic premises did not originate in 1970—the first ordinance dates from 1963. A rapid increase in the supply of new accommodations stabilized rents and the 1963 ordinance was therefore allowed to expire on 30 June 1966. The future will tell whether the 1970 ordinance and subsequent extension are also allowed to expire, or whether they will serve as a foundation for permanent rent controls on domestic and business premises.

The size and cost of the public service have been expanding. Additional manpower will be required to enforce recent labor legislation. Since 1967, no less than 39 items have been passed. Standard working hours for women and young people in industry have been progressively reduced to a maximum of 48 hours a week since 1 December 1971. The Employment Ordinance of 1968 now covers all nonmanual workers whose wages do not exceed HK$1,500 a month and all manual workers in continuous employment. Influenced by International Labor Organization standards, it provides for at least a week's notice or a week's pay in lieu of notice before dismissal, and a measure of wage protection by stipulating that wages must be paid within seven days after they become due. An amendment promulgated in December 1969 provides maternity leave, without pay, for women who have been continuously employed by the same employer for not less than 26 weeks. Another amendment enacted in February 1970 guarantees a minimum of four rest days a month for all workers covered under the ordinance. Prior to the 1969-70 amendments, no restrictions limited hours of work, holidays, or rest periods in the nonindustrial sector. Government has stipulated that neither women nor youths under 18 may be employed underground in a mine, quarry, or tunneling operation. Young persons between 14 and 16 years of age are not permitted

[7] *Annual Report, 1971,* p. 119.

to work overtime in industrial employment and their maximum total working hours are limited to eight hours a day for a six day week Women over 18 and young persons between 16 and 18 are limited to 300 hours overtime per year, not more than 2 hours in any one day. Young persons are barred from night work.[8]

According to England, a number of proposals for additional regulation are currently under discussion in the Labor Department. These include regulation on hours of work, child labor, safety in the whole nonindustrial sector, redundancy payments, and minimum wages. Undoubtedly they include plans for an expansion of the Labor Department staff to cope with the additional regulatory burden.[9] If enacted into legislation and rigorously enforced, these proposals would be a noticeable departure from the colony's tradition of minimal labor regulation, which has been acknowledged for its role in attracting investment. Market forces, not legal restrictions, have been responsible for Hong Kong's high industrial wages. Though the proposals under consideration might protect existing labor, it would most likely do so at the risk of reducing employment opportunities for others by raising wage costs for employers. In any case, if these ordinances and proposals are seriously under consideration, they would constitute visible departures from past policy.

Nor has the government been free from the popular issue of ecology. As the result of a report published in August 1970 by the Committee on Air Pollution in Hong Kong, an Air Pollution Control Unit has been set up which operates under the guidance of the smoke abatement adviser. Seven assistant smoke investigators, though still under training at the end of 1971, were already carrying out field work. Additional regulations for the control of emissions from furnaces, ovens, and chimneys are also in an advanced state of preparation.[10]

The issue of ecology may affect investment and employment. Permission to construct an oil refinery on Lamma Island, just offshore Hong Kong Island, is not to be granted, according to a government announcement, until it can be shown that there will be no harmful effects on the environment. This is typical of the new publicly stated concern for the "quality of life."

---

[8] Ibid., p. 53, and England, "Industrial Relations in Hong Kong," pp. 221–22.
[9] England, "Industrial Relations in Hong Kong," pp. 250–51.
[10] *Annual Report, 1971,* p. 60.

It is readily understood and accepted that government must expend considerable resources providing the necessary infrastructure to facilitate industrial expansion. But how much is required to keep the economy buoyant and thus maintain a steady flow of rising revenue? It is questionable whether the measures discussed in this chapter visibly contribute to economic productivity or enhance public revenues. Indeed, some of them could be counterproductive and scare away investment capital that had in the past been attracted to Hong Kong because of the absence of regulation. Moreover, each of these measures appears somewhat inconsistent with the laissez-faire origins, ideology, and past practices of the Hong Kong government.

What effect these and perhaps still additional measures may have on Hong Kong's economy is difficult to predict for two reasons. First, *government may choose not to enforce much of what it legislates.* This is a question for empirical observation through the 1970s. Second, the continued success of Hong Kong depends, in large measure, on external factors, for example, capital inflow and decisions made in Peking. If, for example, the corruption, incompetence, and inefficiency so prevalent in many Southeast Asian countries continue unabated, then Hong Kong may continue to receive the savings of overseas nationals. Sufficient inroads upon its laissez-faire economic environment may, however, divert part of this capital flow to Singapore. Government's present view is that the resources available now permit welfare measures that hitherto could not be afforded, and also that government now better understands the people's needs and circumstances.[11] The difficulty with this explanation is that it overlooks the costs to the private sector from increased public activity. Although government can better afford to meet the people's "needs" in 1973, it is not evident that public, rather than private, measures will better meet them.

A Restatement of Laissez-Faire

To review the notion of free trade that underlies laissez-faire, the basic idea is that government barriers to competition reduce economic efficiency. The conception asserts that economic activity should take place on the basis of voluntary exchange. The essential conditions

[11] C. P. Haddon-Cave, "The Quality of Life in the Seventies—Government's Continuing Role," a speech delivered to the Hong Kong Management Association on April 7, 1972 (Hong Kong: Government Printer, 1972).

underlying market exchange include: (1) maintenance of law and order by government to prevent the coercion of one individual by another, (2) enforcement of contracts voluntarily entered into, and (3) definition of the meaning of property rights.[12] The belief that laissez-faire cannot exist in a "pure" form because the market system could not function without contractual law is maintained by others.[13] Thus there is an economic justification for at least a minimum of government: the maintenance of an institutional framework within which voluntary exchange can take place. Additionally, defense against foreign enemies that seek to destroy those markets is yet another legitimate public activity. How much more government activity is desired depends on (1) the values that individuals want to maximize, and (2) how well (or poorly) markets free from government control maximize them. A minimum of government seems best suited to maximize economic efficiency and each individual's subjective economic freedom. A much larger government may be necessary to bring about an equal distribution of wealth.

The alleged failure of markets to supply certain kinds of goods known as public goods, that is; items that are in joint supply and which pose problems of excludability, as well as the failure of markets to prevent externalities, has led many to suggest a theory of the state that calls for an ever-growing economic role for government. In this view, not only is the market unable to efficiently allocate those items with public-goods characteristics, it also fails to produce certain desired or needed goods for reasons of technology or cost, and is unable to cope with free-riders. These factors can be used to explain government's monopoly in water works, roads and town planning, and land reclamation. They do not, however, justify interference or control over other private economic activities. The story of Hong Kong's postwar success suggests that a re-emphasis on laissez-faire and a corresponding check on the growth of public activity might contribute to still greater economic growth, and in the long run, to perhaps the average citizen's economic betterment as well. Markets should be allowed to prevail to forestall an increase in below-cost, sometimes arbitrary, and often inefficient public allocation of scarce economic resources.

---

[12] See Milton Friedman, *Capitalism and Freedom* (Chicago and London: University of Chicago Press, 1962), p. 27.

[13] See, for example, Paul Craig Roberts, *Alienation and the Soviet Economy* (Albuquerque: University of New Mexico Press, 1971), p. 54.

The thesis of this study is that the growth of Hong Kong's exceptionally dynamic economy was due, in large measure, to the government's rigid enforcement of a fundamentally hands-off policy toward the private sector. Few places remain where man conducts his economic affairs in an environment of virtually unfettered free enterprise and where officials are free from the public electoral pressures that limit or prevent the application of an economic policy proven successful in twentieth-century Hong Kong. It would be tragic if the well-intentioned welfare policies of the government, rather than uncontrollable external forces, brought about the economic decline of Hong Kong.

Topics for Further Research

Not only does the fact of colonial status make Hong Kong a very special polity, it is, as well, the world's only polity with a legally specified and agreed-upon date of expiration. Enscribed in 1898, Hong Kong's 99-year lease on the New Territories, in which most of the colony's water, energy production, agricultural and industrial output, and half of its population are located, is due to expire in 1997. If the lease is not renewed or renegotiated, the return of the New Territories to Peking removes the economic basis for the continued survival of Hong Kong Island, Kowloon, and Stonecutter's Island, even though these three territories have been ceded to the British in perpetuity. The export earnings from the factories that are situated in the industrial towns throughout the New Territories provide the revenues that pay for Hong Kong's voluminous consumer imports. Loss of these economic assets renders further British presence in Hong Kong precarious. Thus, a first interesting topic for research concerns the future economic welfare of Hong Kong given this impending territorial and economic loss.

If the Chinese remain quiet on the question of renewing the lease, when will the capital inflow begin to taper off? Indeed, when will the inevitable massive capital outflow begin? When will the heretofore politically apathetic Chinese residents strive to outdo each other with xenophobic displays of nationalistic sentiment and hostility toward the colonial rulers in anticipation of takeover by Peking? Hong Kong's prosperity depends on capital inflow. In the absence of it, chronic balance-of-payments deficits would quickly dampen the buoyancy of the local economy and, in the long run, impoverish its citizens. Moreover, past decolonization practices confirm that the British are quick to give up colonies which require subsidies from Britain. At present, the amortization of capital in Hong Kong is complete within three to five years. But, to liquidate one's assets in Hong Kong at their maximum value requires that other potential sellers be outguessed. Businessmen who wait too long to sell may find that their assets have suffered an appreciable decline in market value. Unless the Chinese offer a hint of their policy on the New Territories' lease by 1984, capital inflow will certainly decline sometime during the 1980s and the outflow begin. Possessing a free market in money, Hong Kong has the potential for becoming impoverished within 24 hours. Its past and present economic achievements are, therefore, all the more noteworthy in that they have occurred under this precarious condition. The Chinese decision to renew the lease depends, of course, on whether Hong Kong's continued existence is deemed necessary in order to obtain valuable foreign exchange earnings heretofore considered vital by Chinese economic planners. If the Chinese cannot find or create alternate sources of income, then Hong Kong, with the New Territories intact, may survive well into the twenty-first century.

A second topic for serious study involves the issues raised in this chapter. Will the new publicly financed government programs be detrimental to continued economic prosperity? Or will the Hong Kong economy maintain its dynamic performance despite government's growing economic and regulatory activities? More to the purpose of the political scientist is to account for these recent changes in public policy. Why has the government adopted new programs that represent substantial departures from previous policies? What are the internal or external pressures that underpin these new measures? Are they the result of a conscious choice to increase government's participation in the economy in the belief that these welfare measures will enhance the quality of life in Hong Kong? Or do they represent the views of officials who now assert that government must take the wishes of the population into account, even if substantial intervention in the economy is required, perhaps with some loss in efficiency? Additionally, it will be interesting to ascertain if these new programs are simply window dressing to satisfy popular demand and political pressures or represent, in fact, significant intrusions into the private sector. That is, will government implement and rigorously enforce these new provisions? Finally, might not an increasingly well-educated youth in Hong Kong, even without signals from the mainland, place growing pressures on the anachronistic colonial government, and thereby lessen Hong Kong's attractiveness to overseas investors?

A third possible study could expand upon the political economy framework. How does Hong Kong compare to other units of similar political status in different cultural and geographical settings, for example, Gibraltar and Bermuda? Is it the working of laissez-faire that has brought prosperity to Hong Kong, or is it more directly the propensity to hard work so characteristic of the Chinese? Do other colonial territories practice similar policies of minimum government intrusion in their respective economies? Comparative analysis could extend the validity and reliability of the lesson for economic welfare which this case study of Hong Kong provides.

A last possible study might assess the effect of a future change in the status of Hong Kong on American foreign policy—military, economic, monetary, et cetera. Present American policy toward Hong Kong is pragmatic and business-oriented. The United States government neither supports nor opposes colonial rule in Hong Kong. American policy is simply to assist its citizens who seek to do business in or trade with Hong Kong. When Hong Kong is no longer economically attractive or politically stable, these businessmen will undoubtedly move elsewhere. A change in the political status of Hong Kong, for example, incorporation in the People's Republic of China, would subsume American activities in Hong Kong under the broader rubric of American transactions with China. Before this political change is imminent, barring unforeseen events, most American-owned assets will have been relocated. Since Hong Kong serves no direct military purpose, Chinese takeover poses no security problems for American military planners. The chief value of Hong Kong, apart from the business opportunities it affords, lies in the American consulate's collection of information about mainland China for use by scholars and government officials alike. Abrogation of British rule in Hong Kong might necessitate the establishment of an alternate information network.

Cover and book design: Pat Taylor